The Journey of the Malevolent Empress

The Journey of the Malevolent Empress

A Priestess on a Captivating Journey from Mundane to Magikal

Rev. Gina Micek

Published by Flying Witch Media, Palo Alto, California

www.malevolentempress.com
www.myspace.com/themalevolentempress

While some stories are based on actual experiences with a person either living or dead and on past-life experiences known to the author; the stories have been dramatized or changed for narrative effect and are not intended to be actual representations. This is a work of fiction.

ISBN: 978-0-578-04701-0
Printed in the United States of America

MY REQUEST TO YOU: This book took four years to complete and countless hours of creative juice; please respect this and do not copy or distribute this book without benefit of purchase. If you have friends that would enjoy reading this – please purchase it for them or ask them to purchase it directly. Thank you!

Rev. Gina Micek

Lyrics to "I Dare You," written by Jason Deere & Kristyn Osborn. Used by permission of Alfred Publishng.

All photographs were shot by Abigail Huller, Abigail Huller Photography.

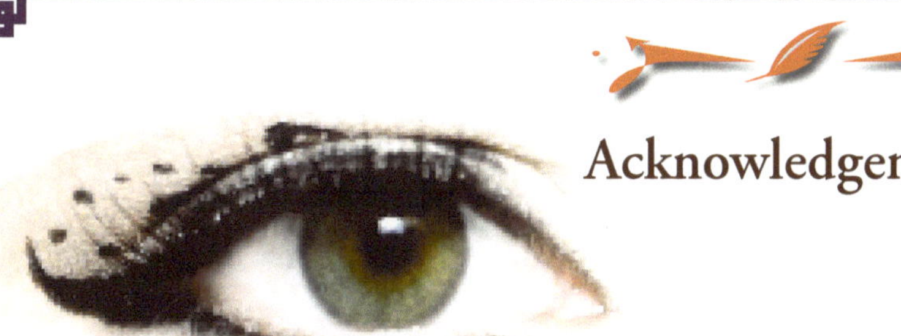

Acknowledgements

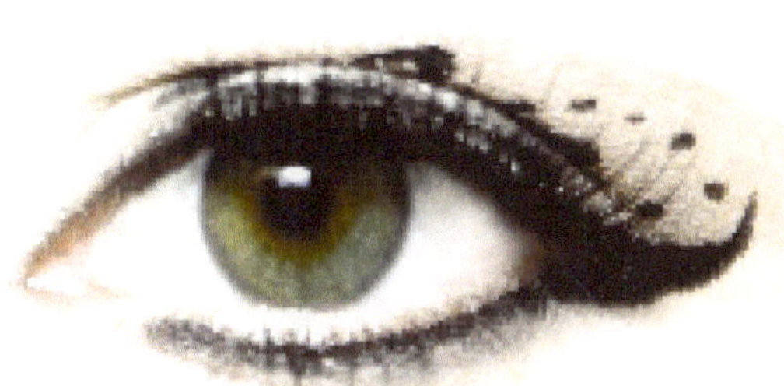

Special Thanks To:

Natasha Lee – my Financial Alchemy/creativity partner who saw me through the ups and downs it took to complete the work.

Mika Stratton -- for stepping in and editing the final drafts - awesome eyes!

CTI(The Coaches Training Institute) -- for their wonderful coaching program

Deena Metzger – whose writings aided in my initiation as a healer and whose dedication to fostering indigenous mind lent itself to my own brand of creative output.

Clive Prout, CPCC – who helped me look under the microscope for the positive magnificence while I wore the red dress

David Rich – the first musician I had a personal relationship with at the age of five -- we have to start somewhere with these things -- listening to you play your instrument in person was a defining moment as was knowing your father Leighton whose life was music -- thanks for reading my poetry!

All the teachers at the Correllian Tradition and WitchSchool – your dedication to fostering Wiccan education for all led me through this awesome, awe-inspiring journey with Spirit.

All my art and writing teachers -- for helping to hone my craft.

My ancestors and Spirit Guides – for never giving up!

Find the Music Within...

Amy Julianna Brassfield

You connected to me with your Heart
In a moment of Grace

Which opened up in me
A pathway yet unseen

In perfect love
And perfect Trust

You helped me FINISH IT!

Belovéd Amy
My friend in Spirit

Dedication

Joseph Alexander Paymar

There is a word in Ojibwe which means "All Things"
Don't ask me how I know this --
Drummer, Shaman, Father,
Brother, Son, Lover, Friend --
It speaks to timelessness in relationships which never end.

You found my soul in the Underworld through your drums and brought me back to music, to inspiration.
In turn, I loved enough to find you in your darkness and return you to the light.
Our broken relationship is now whole, complete
We can rejoice for now we will never be lost again.
I know you will write a new Story, my friend.
One of joy, creative spirit, perseverance through adversity & natural beauty in abundance.
We are in each other's hearts forever...

Contents

Contents

A Witch & her Familiar

Forward

What a journey! I began this project in February of 2005 thinking when I began I would be done in a few months. I was wrong. Many twists and turns and seasons would have to transpire before the project came together. The Story as it stands took its own time to develop and, in the end, was not up to me other than to be receptive to the process.

The journey of a Priestess – maybe in the time before King Arthur, the burning times or the many lifetimes of living in hiding, we Pagans understood this journey. We had teachers. We had acceptable pathways to serving the Goddess. The pathways were lost. Obscured. Obliterated. Tortured. Burned.

We lost more than a way of life. Both men and woman lost a compass to a compassionate heart. We no longer knew how to love ourselves let alone the planet or each other yet we needed this involution time, this darkness to learn lessons of strength and perseverance; to improve our mental acuity, to evolve our technology, science and expand our awareness on all levels.

Now, I am happy to say, the time has come again for the Priest and Priestess -- spiritual people who hold space for healing and enable new, more wholistic thought patterns to enter the culture. Communities need us, individuals, definitely so, and the Universe more than ever.

We see beyond limits. We understand the nature of spiritual journey having clearly taken one ourselves. We don't know "everything;" we aren't Gods, what we are is heart open to the endless mystery of life. The mystery never ends.

My journey will continue, of course. It's nice once in awhile, however to take some time out and celebrate how far one has come. The publication of this book is that moment for me. I have dedicated this book to an individual without whom the journey would not have taken place in its entirety. He was clearly sent by Goddess to do her work in my life. And then also in memory of someone whose story helped me "Finish It..." -- a line taken from a wonderful movie about the journey of lifetimes called "The Fountain."

There were numerous others on this road – not mentioned here but no less worthy. Each person has their place, their lesson, their spiritual purpose. Needless to say, if you met me once, you taught me something. I hope you enjoy the results.

To my Circle – my mailing list and MySpace friend list – your love, attention, and community Spirit are both inspirational and humbling. A writer I could not be, without the gift of your presence.

To others on the journey from mundane to magikal – we are on the path together – hang in there. You are not alone...even when the path feels empty.

To the musicians and music fans from The Sweetwater, Sweetwater Station and other venues, you inspire everything in me I may be a Priestess in your presence, however, your gifts and devotion challenge me to continually expand my thinking and my creativity.

Where this journey ends, another begins. I look forward to the horizons and crossroads yet to come. The journey is forever a worthy one.

Love & Light -- Rev. Gina Micek

October 31st, 2008 (Samhain)

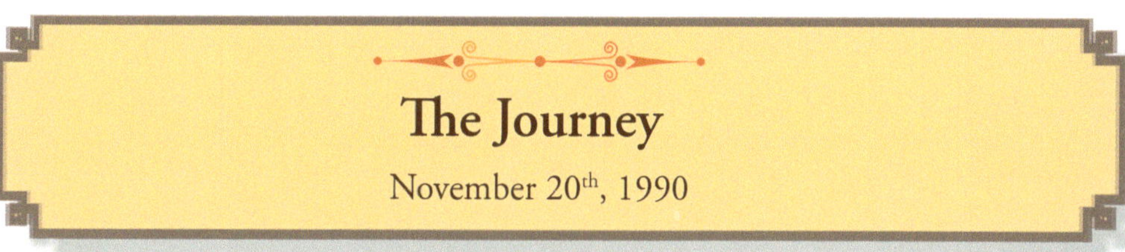

The Journey

November 20th, 1990

God came to me one day and said He had found me a home. I told Him I did not need one because He was a good father and I was not going to leave.

God said to me, "Now I have always taken care of you."

"Right," I agreed.

"You know I will always be there, wherever you are."

"Right," I nodded.

"It is time for you to leave me and make someone very happy. They will take care of you as I have."

"I'm not sure about this," I said.

"Look," God said, and He pointed and I saw.

There was a man and a woman and they loved each other. I could tell because of the way they gazed into each other's eyes across the dinner table and caressed each other's hands.

"They have been praying for a child," He said to me, "I think you should be the one."

"I'm scared," I quivered, my voice trembling. "What if they don't like me? Can I come back to you?"

"Now, now," He said and laid a hand on my shoulder. "I love you with all my being and cherish you like you were my only child. I will only tell you the truth. You cannot return once you have gone to that place until you have lived the life you were meant to live. The World is not like this place here. It has a right and a wrong. It has a bad and a good. But you can choose."

"What do you mean?"

"There will be things called, "Temptations,"" He said, "these temptations will call to you and there will be things called, "Necessities" and they will call to you. It will be difficult to tell the difference sometimes but you must choose."

"This sounds hard," I said matter-of-factly.

God replied, "Sometimes you will go on a path that leads nowhere or goes in circles."

"What do I do when that happens?"

"You try to find the way out."

"I'll miss you," I conceded.

"Oh, Child! I will always be there."

"Can I call you whenever I want?"

"I will always listen," He assented.

"When do I go?" I asked.

"Now," He said. And in a blinding flash of light I felt myself falling and I cried out. I feared greatly that He had not heard me and I reached back for Him, groping the air. He grasped me and I stopped falling for a moment. His voice thundered in my ear.

"One day you will be able to return and once again sit at my side and live in peace. May this forever be your guide in life and may Faith always stay in your soul." As His voice died, I felt His hand let go of me and I tumbled into the dark abyss.

I was BORN and she held me near her breast. Her heart thumped and I heard God again, in my mind.

"You are their child now and they will raise you. Remember always that I love you."

She told me how pretty I was and she played with my toes. She held me close and she made me stop crying when I felt homesick.

"I love her," I felt with all my being as I cannot speak as yet. She held my hands when I wanted to walk on limbs that seemed too shaky to hold me up. She held my head when I got sick and threw up in a bowl. Later, she pushed me onto the school bus even though I did not really want to go to school.

I spoke to God again today. It has been awhile. He does not seem to answer like He used to and I am scared. I do have faith that He listens. I told Him how she hurt me and I wanted to go back to live with Him. She spanked me because I left my younger brother in someone else's backyard. He was being such a pain. I do not understand why they got him and I cannot believe he has ever really lived with God. I guess I'll just have to figure this out on my own; I do not hear Him say anything. I can only feel this pain in my heart.

The kids were awful to me at school today; they said I wore funny clothes. I cried and she comforted me and said that everything would be all right one day. I've heard that before but I do not remember where.

I do not believe in God any longer. I'm a teenager now and I know better than Mom and everyone what is real and what is not. People at Church say to have faith and that is such a load of baloney. What do they know anyway because why would a God that loves us allow little kids to suffer or for there to be poor people. It is so lame.

A man offered me something today and he said it would make me feel good. I was going to try it but then a word flashed in my head, "Temptation." Where have I heard about this before? I shook my head to get that vision out, probably some lame thing some old biddy said in Church. I tried the stuff anyway. Man! I did feel good. Real good.

Later, I had more and more of the stuff and I started feeling bad again. My body hurt. I wanted to die. I ran to her again. She held me close when I could hardly stand anymore – only pain and longing raged through my body.

I saw Him standing before me; I had forgotten. He smiled and said He loved me and that I would be okay. He said I could have peace now, if I wanted. I could feel the pain and all I wanted was to be myself again.

I looked over at her. Tears were running down her cheeks and fear was apparent in her eyes. "She loves me," I thought, like He does. Now I remember Him telling me there would be choices. He said there would be bad things in my life as well as good. I have a choice now, to stay or go back. Again He asked if I wanted to come with Him.

"I love you with all my heart," I tell him, "but I love her too, in a different way. She cries because she fears I will not return. I do not want to hurt her." He started to fade but before He left completely He said something important.

"You have made a difficult choice – to feel pain and live life – but I give you the strength to endure. You have found the door."

I graduated high school. Not summa cum laude, or anything. She cried. She cries at everything, I swear. I did not see her in the crowd while I shook the principal's hand and got my diploma. I knew she was proud, though. I felt her eyes on me.

I said, "God, I made the right choice didn't I?" Although I could not hear His answer directly, I felt His presence with me that day as well.

Time passes and I sit in my dorm room. She is at home. I know she worries. I want to tell her I love her and will never go away again. I want to tell her how happy I am. It is hard though, making choices. Deciding what is right and what is wrong. I get tempted a lot these days. Some days I feel really bad and I see God again like I saw Him that day when I realized I was an addict and was going to die if I didn't choose life. He smiles and says nothing. I see her crying and feel her sadness and know I could never do that stuff again.

I pray to Him everyday and ask Him for strength to get me through to the next morning. I dream one night of a beach with a set of footprints. They are too big to be mine. In the dream I know it is because He is carrying me.

My goal is to be a famous writer and communicate my thoughts about Him to the world. I hope to make her proud. I think about the day I will go to live with God again and I know I have everything to live for now.

Defiance, Required

Naked in the Rain

If you knew my secrets
My life would not end
My life would begin

I feel the raindrops
On my naked body
Cold and light

They make my senses reel
Everything finely tuned
Like Mozart on a violin

I'll tell you that I walked outside
Without my clothes on
I could never have done this before

They protected me
Separated me from myself
From the world

And I liked it that way
No feeling
No hurt

The layers grew
I shiver now but am not cold
Raindrops bathe me in warmth

Awareness is full
You know my secrets
I have nothing to hide

I am whole
Darkness ebbs from my toes
Taken by the light

Emanating like a halo
Surrounding me
Crucifying death

Before I'd hide
Now I shout to the world
As my feet squelch the wet grass

Mud pushes out between my toes
"I know now what it feels like to run naked in the rain!"

1992

Jungle Voices

(Reflections on Paul Simon's "Spirit Voices")

I

Jungle breathes contiguous green
Follow the
Rhythm
Rhythm beating
Booming echo
Of the jungle
Drumming—

Through boundaries
Heavy foliage
Circle of lights
Hum of the gathering
Passion connects
Music dreaming worlds
Seething body's harmony

Entering the circle
Air charred embers
Green leaves
Spirit voices speaking
Floating in suspension
The spirit voices singing

Passion fills our hearts
The night
Telling stories
Spinning tales of centuries
Voices
Undulating
Our spirits un-delineated

From the milieu
Dancing
Breathing the universe in
Through our mouths
Sheltering from common sorrow

II

River moves us
Back through the black
Stars
Our hearts moving inside
In rhythm
With the whole
Sounds burst and wane

The baby's screams
The men's joking
And the spirit voices.
Echo against the rocks
Our ancestor's singing
From their mossy houses
Deep in the night

February 13th, 1994

Love In London

I

Bar on New Year's Eve
Pink neon sign flashing
Thonged and tasseled dancers
Sliding on poles, in cages

Bathed in orange light
Hot bodies woven
Tight pack of skin flesh,
Short skirts, knee boots

Flannel caps and roving eyes
Slick-chested barman
Muscles sinuous bumps
White straight smile

Women serving, see through
To black silkies, tight butts
Low cut sequin tops
Baby fuzzed men longing looks

Desperate coy smiles
Compact boy muscles flexing
Under Lycra cycling shorts
Undefined cheekbones wide doe eyes

II

Hands resting on my hips
We twist to the floor
Viewing multiple pairs of shoes
Shuffling to the beat

Hot breath on my neck
Numbness in my brain
Sipping white diamonds
Hands slide gently down

My back over my breasts
Shallow breathing stomach
Tightens warmth flows
Through my inner thigh

Sweaty palms clasped we dance
Hot breath on my face
Sticky tongue probing

Biting, caressing with his teeth
Tiny stiff hairs on his face
Scratching movement of his jaw

III

Ears ringing in hazy night
"Happy New Year!"
Eating onion covered hotdogs
Holding them so the ketchup doesn't run out

Clasping his knees with my legs
In empty trashed Trafalgar Square
Head on his shoulder
Alleviating my exhaustion

IV

Hours before dawn
Our breath condensed white
Hands numb tongue burned by coffee
From Styrofoam cup

He goes home on the bus
Leaving me with a cold
Man with a broom
Sweeps bright colored flyers

Where they've collected
On the stairs to the Underground,
Singing softly to himself

V

Sleeping cramped
Friend's hotel room
Tiny single bed
Wreaking of smoke

Unhooked jeans,
Bodysuits too complicated fasteners
Lumpy money belt sticking in my rib
A brain stuffed in skull

Swimming with kisses
Sweaty people bumping
Neon sign marking way down
To those dancing girls

January 1995

No Name

Jaunty
Morning sun
In my eyes

Strolling
To the sound of
Dusky jazz

Groovin' tunes
Atmospheric blues
Smile

Teeth gleaming white
Maybe you forgot
To hate me --

Clash!
Play a little harder

Funky tap dance
Flip, flop

Dancing on the street
Commercial for soup

Bubbles
And then –

You make it up to me
Fingering my heart

Strangeness
Consummate professional

Pick my song, huh?

January 5, 2006

Dances in Freedom

Ordinary Ghosts

I am with the plumber. We're lying in his bed. He is having sex with me. To tell you the truth the whole thing is not that interesting. In fact, it is just plain ordinary. Not like when I was sixteen years old and I imagined being in bed with all those hunks that my girlfriends and I giggled over in magazines.

Remember them? For my generation -- River Phoenix, Johnny Depp, members of New Kids on the Block and Matt Dillon. I do not think it matters which generation you are in – you have someone in mind you can put in the picture. These guys grace the covers of the teen magazines and represent the perfect man. Now I think, why are we fooling ourselves here? River Phoenix turned out to be a junkie. Anyway, for a moment in time, these guys were the ones we wanted. The ones we wanted but did not see on our high school campus anywhere. Those boys were just boys and most of them uninterested in us anyway.

The high school boys had braces, acne and smelled bad. The men in those magazines and in those movies we spent hours watching, knew exactly what to say, when it say it and oh, yeah, they knew how to kiss. Kissing always led to sex. I can tell, your morality shackles are up – maybe you are watching too many of those teen movies they make these days. The teen movies where teens actually have sex on camera and know exactly what to do. We were not that sophisticated. I am wondering, is anyone that sophisticated?

Late at night, after bedtime, when the homework was done, I would imagine Johnny Depp entering my front door, knowing exactly what to say and do. He would kiss me and I would respond with moans and go limp in his arms. Soon after, we would somehow end up in my bedroom with my parents completely out of the picture – where did they go anyway? Did they even care that their sixteen-year-old daughter was taking a man upstairs alone while they watched "Roseanne" on TV? Maybe they were not aware?

Johnny and I would make passionate love and I would scream in ecstasy. Substitute my circling, frantic, frenetic fingers for Johnny's rather large, completely sophisticated penis. I would get bored of this fantasy after a few nights and go onto other dreams. The fantasy gets boring because after awhile you realize that you are alone eating lunch on the high school campus and no one is remotely interested in one iota of your real life, let alone kissing you passionately and knowing exactly what to say and do. Who the fuck knows what to say and do?

Fast forward, I am in bed with the plumber (substitute any lackluster partner of yours). For me, it is my first time. I am in my early twenties and I have determined that I am past due. "I just need to get over the hump," I tell myself. Here I am in bed getting fucked. Except "getting fucked" is the biggest letdown of my life. After Johnny and River, who the hell wants this middle-aged plumber with a beer belly, two kids and a nasty divorce he cannot stop talking about?

I try to be happy. I smile a lot even after the umpteenth time he asks me, "Are you sure you are alright, it's really tight down there, maybe this is hurting you?"

I also repeat for the umpteenth time, "No, this is exactly how I imagined it, everything is great!"

The truth -- I want to bolt. I am ready to take my virginity back and stay that way. Maybe I will become a nun and devote myself to helping poor children somewhere? Maybe I will just die.

I want to love the plumber. Isn't that what happens? I fall in love. There is happiness in my life. The plumber, the one I am losing my virginity with, embodies the perfect partner, the one who will whisk me away from all the choices that are too difficult to make myself. Life will be easier?

The actuality is, in the entirety of our short-lived, obviously doomed relationship, I never once feel satisfied. I give myself orgasms, usually after he has fallen asleep. He never asks and I never demand. The few times I try to

communicate my needs, the little pecker he calls Fred is not up to task.

"Is it in there?" I ask.

"Sure, baby, can't you feel it?"

His beer belly bumps against my pelvic bone in an attempt to reinforce his point. I cannot answer – truthfully.

All I think is...no one told me to ask for more than this?

I am a lost soul. One of the many -- lost and forgotten. I hardly know my talents and none are realized. I sent all the plumber's ridiculous belongings back to him. The ring that he bought me on credit -- the one that later causes his credit card to decline at dinner one night. The photos of us in "happy" moments. Moments created so I can finally say I have a boyfriend like everyone else and finally lose my virginity like everyone else. I also gave him a few things I now wish I had back. The plumber is not my problem now; I could care less.

I am in my therapist's office looking at all the figurines she has on shelves. Mythical knights and damsels, dragons. Nurses, doctors. Animals. She has so many. They are used in the sandbox. The sandbox as a tool does not interest me in the least. You have been out of my life for eight months and the reason I am here is because I would rather be dead. What good are the fairy tales to me now? They mean diddly-squat; the story makes no sense. Nothing makes sense. Right now, right this minute; the only thing that will work to save my life is the absolute, unshakable understanding that you are going to come back. I am here in this therapy chair talking and my mind takes me into these memories as though the situations are happening again right this minute. The day we met in person, I was a lost soul. One of the many. One who believed she had been found.

You are sitting in your forest green truck messing with the dial on the radio. I can just make out your close-cropped red hair and your manly hand on the steering wheel. We agreed to spend the day together after our Internet chats and phone calls suggested something in common. I am running late for our date and annoyed because my pedicure appointment ran long. I am completely unprepared to meet you. As many young women do, I imagined I'd be able to run out quickly in sweats get my nails done and have plenty of time to take a shower, do hair, make-up and get dressed in something tasteful but alluring. A concept requiring impeccable timing, which went terribly wrong on this day.

I am running from my car, in sweats trying to slip by unnoticed in order to take care of these minor details like a shower but you are too quick. Before I know what has happened, I am nervously opening the front door with you right next to me while making excuses for keeping you waiting. I wear no make-up and my outfit is less than alluring.

I think -- this has to be the worst moment of my life! I am mortified. Here you are, larger than life gorgeous. You actually have muscles under that shirt and are wearing your jeans like a glove. The man from the movies on my doorstep, Exhibit A. I, on the other hand am late, disheveled and sick to my stomach.

Later, after I hurriedly make myself decent, we get into your truck and drive to Santa Cruz but not before we head to the convenience store to get snacks in case I am thirsty or hungry - no one has ever thought to take care of me in this way before.

On the road you play Garth Brook's "Shameless" over and over on the CD player. It's a terribly romantic song and the words speak to a head-over-heels connection, which I might just be feeling.

Jeez do you have to be that good? Do you have to know exactly what to say and in that southern accent too?

I feel like I have gone to sleep and woken up as Molly Ringwald in the movie "Sixteen Candles."

We spend the day together wandering around my old college town while I explain how things have changed and what I love about downtown. You actually seem to care and listen to everything I say, which is a drastic change from all the men and most of the people I have ever known. We seem to fit, you and I; it's like I am meeting my other half and melting into a dream. Sure there are nerves and mis-steps but none of these matter right? The perceptions of perfection must be correct. This is how I choose to remember that day anyway. How do you remember our first meeting?

Day turns into evening. We decide to see a movie everyone is bragging about. We both decide we are not as thrilled as the rest of America. How wonderful it is to meet someone who feels the same way I do about things. The next stop on your Santa Cruz tour is the beach; it's already dark out and you still want to go. You thought the beach would be closer to where I live and planned to sleep there overnight when I went home! I point out the numerous signs that read – "No sleeping on the beach" -- as we head down from the parking lot onto the sand and take our walk along the ocean.

We are laughing about this small fact of inconvenience as we carry your sleeping bag to the shore so we can enjoy the sound of the surf crashing, the moonlight streaming down and the warmth of each others' bodies as we hold hands. The feel of you next to me as you wrap your arms around me sends shivers through my spine and warmth circulating up my center despite the chill of the ocean breeze. I cannot imagine being anywhere but with you at this moment. How can you be so perfect?

I lay on top of you in that sleeping bag, the taut muscles of your legs pressing into my body, your arms around my waist so secure and confident that I feel like I am wrapped in a cacoon of safety. I walked into my own romance novel on the day I met you and I don't want to leave this book! We kiss and I am thrilled each kiss is a present from heaven. We laugh – about everything. You are nothing like my ex-boyfriend – worried that I am not satisfied, you tell me you will not even hear of taking any from me until I feel complete. We spend the night together in some motel and I do not bother calling home. Mom freaks. I fall in love. Yes -- finally.

The next few months of our burgeoning relationship are sadly spent long distance. You are stationed in California with the military and I am in grad school in Florida. We talk on the phone nightly, sometimes all night. We play multi-player computer games and hang out in chat rooms typing back and forth about our lives until the sun comes up outside my dorm window. I imagine us getting married because after all, you fit the description of the perfect supportive partner. Everyone always said, "You'll know when you have met the one, you'll feel it." I definitely do.

Months into our relationship, you reveal one night that you have a secret you need to tell me -- you were once married and you have a daughter who is two. I struggle to reconcile my picture of the perfect man with the real one in my life telling me these truths. In penance you send flowers and beg me to forgive you for the secrets. I do not have to try too hard to love you; the perfect man is back in all his romantic glory. I keep the "I'm sorry" card from the bouquet.

All the moments, all the truth as I remember it floods my mind like cascading waterfalls of time and space. All the memories – like Christmas spent with your sister in Oregon. We take pictures of ourselves with our arms stretched outward and mock fear on our faces as we pretend to fall off the bridge near her house. The night we spend in Key West when the image of the perfect man gives way to the reality I cannot bear. I hold you tightly as we watch the tropical waves crash against the pier where we sit. Taking in the humid, salty air; I try to cling onto you for warmth not because it is cold out but because I am chilled to the bone from this experience. I think I know what is coming and I do not want to face the truth. The ending. The six months of our relationship that feels this moment like six years. We argue this night in Key West about something stupid. Something my mother tells me I should require of you. I have no idea what to require of love. What is love exactly?

I am in the therapist's chair and she asks me a question that jogs me away from these daydreams or nightmares, depending on your point of view. Prompted by her question, I start telling her about the day you broke up with me. You received your orders to go overseas and call me that week to break-up...

"But I love you," I say.

"Sometimes, love isn't enough," you answer.

I can tell you are trying to get off the phone as quickly as possible. All that comes to my mind while I stall to keep you on the phone longer is:

"This can't be happening, he's perfect."

My psyche fights with the image, the one I want so badly of the knight on the white horse coming to rescue me from a childhood of dashed dreams and all the times my family has made me feel as though I cannot make a decision to save myself. The times too numerous to mention when I am told how every decision I make is a wrong direction I will regret later including this relationship with you I defend constantly.

"You can do it, I believe in you," you write on my birthday card a month after that night on the beach. After the break-up call though you return none of my cries for help. I come up a against a brick wall of reality. I am bruised and battered; questioning everything. Are you really leaving me for good?

I fade back into the little brown therapy room with the memories sliding away from me like water over slimey rocks, salty tears dripping down my face onto my shirt. I tell the therapist I honestly feel I cannot live without you – might as well not live -- I can't imagine there ever will be another man like you.

Nothing that happened during the break-up call makes any sense in my version of reality. The end of the teen movies comes too early to show how to handle what happens next when the guy finds someone else or has to take a job in another state. Here I am, the one who thought she was saved and I am lost once again – adrift on a sea of confusing, dark, unhappy shrunken thoughts. Will someone out there -- anyone -- please tell what I am supposed to do now?

I fight with God because God gave me an imagination; I used it to imagine you as perfect. The fragments of the shattered glass of my illusion lay littered at my feet. I do not need a sandbox to tell me that my perception of reality, in this case, is a fairy tale of my own making. The session ends each week and the story never does. The ball of tissues goes in the trash. My love keeps flowing with nowhere to go. I get up from the therapist's chair and I walk to my car. My destiny is elsewhere and the path lies out of reach.

Seven years since the therapist's chair where I spoke about an ending. What I discover is the moment you left was actually a beginning rather than an end -- the complete annihilation of the illusion I created to make life more meaningful led me on a journey of discovery from which an authenticity is revealed in its entire splendor. Who knew that life could be so stunning? A life so filled with experiences, which are like vibrant color displays of vivid imagination – anything that you desire is possible and yet, unlike my original attempts held up by a crumbling foundation, I

am building something strong and unshakable.

I am on the edge of wakefulness and sleep. The precipice where you can choose to continue to stay awake or simply let go and head to oblivion. That is where I am now with my foot warmer keeping my feet toasty and my dog muffling in his sleep lying next to me. Just there in that space I hear a voice,

"You must go to him."

I feel a rough hand on my back urging me forward with an urgent pressure. I find myself outside your old apartment near the Air Force base. There are kid's toys taking up space on the walkways and the sound of a football game blaring from a television set through an open window. I walk up to a door and open it. The place is empty and abandoned.

"Not this one," the voice reverberates in my ear.

I head down and try another set of stairs. A girl's toy baby buggy stands abandoned on the balcony next to the front door.

I knock. I look over to the blind covering the sliding glass door and the barrel of a gun is pointed at me. What the hell kind of reception is this? You move to open the front door just a crack. One of those little chain bolts prevents my further entry. I call your name.

"What do you want?" you blurt the question roughly and without feeling or ceremony.

Your face in the doorway appears as an impassible wall, your eyes reflect nothing, least of all empathy or compassion. Your hand moves the gun you hold in readiness and perhaps to emphasize your point of view. The air of hostility is self-evident. What am I doing here?

Haltingly, I attempt an explanation. My words sound hollow like I am speaking over some gaping abyss into nothingness. I just want to talk and have no harm in mind. I ask you to let me inside. Your daughter's curiosity gets the better of her just as your defenses are distracted, giving her opportunity to worm her face around your leg and take a peek through the crack in the door. Her cherubic face lights up.

"Mommy, is that you?" she asks matter-of-factly.

I am a little floored. The observation is unexpected.

"She recognizes me," I say half as a question and half knowing that she would.

Children know things and this one knows more than most. You close the door. I have lost. No, wait. I hear the sound of the chain and the door opens once again, wide and almost inviting. Your little girl runs out from behind you, jumping into my arms. She rests her head on my shoulder, with her soft, curly brown hair bouncing against my chin. She wraps her little arms around my neck and grabs a lock of my hair, plying the strands between her fingers. My emotions get the better of me. Tears slide gently down my cheeks and I am lost in the reverie of pure love. A slight movement jogs me to the present and I look up, noticing the curiosity on your face.

"I'm different," I say as if in explanation. "Time has passed, I have grown up and I think, so have you. I came to talk. I want to heal the past and look forward to the future."

You nod curtly and motion for me to enter the room, distrust and unease slowly beginning to dissipate from your being like molasses dripping from a spoon. The living room appears as it once did as though nothing has changed. The brown couch, the gun rack, the stuffed animals including the ones I left there by mistake. We travel the rift of time, after all and so while our spirits have developed, the scene remains the same. This space is where I knew you and where I will know you again. I wonder briefly where you reside now and realize just as quickly that the answer has no bearing on my time with you.

A little shaken, I feel it necessary to fill the void by explaining the past life that brought me here in the first place. Your little girl, the one staring back at me so inquisitively at this moment is my daughter from another lifetime. A place in time long ago where I died in childbirth, never really knowing how she faired. The bonds of love between her and I were so powerful and the severing of our cord, so abrupt that my spirit went to the other side suffering in the pain of unanswered questions. I explain that in that lifetime, my family had lied to me about their plans with regard to my pregnancy and the situation ended tragically. You seem to accept this, as I knew you would.

We used to converse, you and I about past lives and conjecture on the little memories, the tiny fragments and feelings, which gave us some ideas about what those lives may have entailed. I was not adept or trained in those days in meditation or psychic work. I did not think, as I do now about the big picture or go into trance to learn about the shared history of lifetimes with the people I now know. The talk was just novelty and possibility. I remember you being convinced that you had once been a Native American because you were drawn to those images and sounds, the stories of the Old West. What conversations we would have now since these concepts would be so much more real to me. I am relieved to see that she, the one I lost, who is your daughter now, is healthy and happy. You are a good father and she is well cared for.

We sit down on your couch. Thankfully, you replace the gun in your gun rack. You'd bought the rack at the local thrift store, which I remember you proudly showing off the day you bought it, wondering why anyone would give up something so great. I smile despite myself.

"What happened with us?" I ask. "I know for my part, I was naïve about love, I wanted to believe you were the perfect man, when in reality you were just a man. And for holding you on a pedastal you could never reach I am truly sorry."

You look at me, as you used to, steely brown eyes, seeing past the layers of my skin and bone, right into the center of my soul.

"I was scared, " you admit. "I knew I had to leave my daughter with her mother while I went overseas and I worried that something was going to happen to her, since I believed my ex neglected and abused her. So I hired that private investigator, you know her name?"

I nod, momentarily squeezing my eyes shut while remembering the emails and instant messages I received from a woman who tortured me long after you were gone with carefully crafted notes aimed at searing my heart and tearing the competition, as she saw it, to pieces. One line in particular comes to mind and I take a breath, drawing air through my teeth as if the sheer effort will dull the pain. "He doesn't love you and never did." My body is filled with the crest of emotion.

"I made a terrible mistake," you continue, looking down at your fingernails and fidgeting in the cushion. "I thought I could use her to keep tabs on my ex while I was overseas and to gather any information I needed to appeal for custody. I realized how big a mistake I made when my sister informed me what she was up to with you. She was difficult to get rid of after that." I can tell the memories tear at you and you breathe in deeply, your jaw tight -- the proverbial cowboy with a weight on his shoulders. I look over at you.

"It was hard for me to reconcile all the good times we shared together with that person who wouldn't answer my calls, cut me off without another word and let that woman say all those things she said. I remained tortured about it for a long while, running the memories in circles in my mind and nothing good came from that struggle. It wasn't until I worked with someone, a therapist, and looked at all the family dynamics and old pains and hurts that any of it made sense."

You look me straight in the eye now. Even in this place, with all its astral strangeness, its dreamy, soft-edged quality, I can tell something big is about to happen.

"I definitely was not perfect. I had made a lot of mistakes in my life up to that point, and many of them cost me dearly. The worst mistake I ever made was telling you I never loved you. I loved you so deeply it hurt but I was just too damn scared to do the right thing. I knew on some level you were better off without me. You had important

things to accomplish and being with me at that moment wasn't one of them. But I could have figured out another way."

I shake my head in disbelief. How do you read my thoughts so well? Tears slide softly and salty into my mouth. So I was correct in my absolute belief that your letter, signed officially with an Air Force signature was either not you or not you being truthful. I put my hand on your arm and draw it down, maternally caressing your arm until I clasp your hand in mine.

"But sweetheart," I say, "even though it killed me inside and I thought for years that some mistake had been made by the Universe, your act of leaving, of abandoning me the way you did, was the best thing that could have happened to me. From that moment on my true healing began. Now I am at a place in my life where I am finally starting to feel strong and whole."

I smile at you and look deeply into your eyes, the doorway to your soul, to the place where we are just true essence, not body, bone or skin but pure white light. Love and joy radiate around us. You return my gaze, your mouth upturned, just slightly. The tension falls from your body and you relax, tautness replaced with a lighter, more fluid energy, like a cascading waterfall.

"I finally realized that what occurred came from a place of such deep love that you were willing to put your own desires, your life, your wish not to hurt me to the side, and do what was most difficult," I continue. "I believe we made this arrangement, you and I, before incarnating on the planet. You did it for me, so I could learn the important lessons, grow as a soul and become a better human being. I am who I am because of you and I thank you for it."

I look at you intensely now and add, "I too, had a part to play in our demise. I was so lost. I held you up on a pedestal and asked you to support me at the same time. I asked you to give me what I could not give myself – a sense of self and self love. I asked for validation and my well was never filled. That is too much to ask of one person. The moment you needed me to support you, I could not, even then I asked, 'How am I going to survive without him?' I never once asked you what I could do for you when you had to leave your daughter so long."

I held both his hands now, their warmth in this place, let me know the bond of love between us was still strong and would remain forever that way as we continued with our lives.

"I am not afraid to meet you in person," I say gingerly, "I once was afraid, I thought the situation, the feelings would be the same. I did not think I could bear to see your face. I would love with no return, I would feel shame and hurt. I would repeat the ending again, like some bad joke."

"But you know so much more than you did then," you say to me matter-of-factly, a broad smile illuminating your face. "You and I would meet and we would have all this life that has happened to us, all this wisdom and we are two people, grown more wise, more mature, right?"

I can remember how you used to have just the right words for any moment. Your ability to say what mattered is one of the things I loved about you; still do love about you. Here we both are in your old apartment, as though nothing has changed, and yet everything is different.

"I got custody, you know," you say looking at your daughter with great love and admiration. Your daughter is playing with her trucks on the floor and looks up at us smiling. "She lives with me now and I thank God for that everyday."

"She once was mine and now she is yours. You better take care of her very well," I say, smirking in your direction. You smile and nod in affirmation. I am wistful now because I think we cannot stay forever in this place between the worlds. We have this opportunity to heal something between us and yet we have lives to lead and so I know our meeting must come to end, for now.

"It is almost time for me to go," I say.

"We both did our best with what we had at the time," you add, "we are here so we can agree we would do it dif-

ferently now and yet, then is all we have."

"I agree that we have this moment to see things differently and create a new feeling between us, one where we have both received the answers we need and can finally, finally heal the wounds."

Overwhelmed with emotion, I lean forward to kiss you on the lips. We meet there and the warmth and electricity of true love flows between us. There is no need for fairy tales and skewed visions in this place where only love is real. We hold each other tightly, as we used to do, yet this time, I have no fear of losing you because now I know I never will.

I stand, for now I know the time arrives when I must depart this space, the walls become fuzzy and the sound of buzzing gets louder.

"I love you," I say, "and my love for you will never end. We will meet again, you and I, either in this life or somewhere on the other side when this lifetime is complete. I hope we do bump into each other with these bodies, I look forward to it and wish for it and yet if we never meet in person again, I know that I have found you, just as I have found myself."

You take your daughter's hand now. I kneel down on the floor and place my fingers in her curly mop. Love flows from her brown doe eyes and she falls into my arms, her quiet breathing hot against my cheek.

"You guys take care of each other, I'll see you soon."

I look for a long time into her face every detail etched into memory so that recalling her will always be easy. I stand and we head towards your door, a door now glowing brightly with the light of the summer place.

"Until we meet again," he says.

And I step into the light.

I awake deep in the dark of night, moonlight flooding in my window, casting shadows through the room where I sleep -- alone. My body wracks with sobs. Tears stream like warm pillows down my cheeks. My bed warmer is long cold. How much time passed, I do not know. The clock is fuzzy. My heart beats in rhythm and yet there is warmth there, something beyond myself still lingers like fingers caressing my skin or the touch of God. Being in the place between the worlds forever changes me. I am struck with the power of it and yet, my mundane self still yearns for some personal flesh on flesh touch. I grasp the pillow as if my action might reveal the feeling of your skin beneath my hands and the warmth of your body next to mine.

I am still amazed at the powers I have developed to meet in the world between worlds and interact with the spirits of the living and of the dead. And yet, there are times when I long for life to be ordinary, simple and understood. Like the fairy tales I created to make life easier when real life got to be too much. The story I created about you, which left me feeling as if I was in control and which once seemed so real, doesn't quite add up like it used to. Those fairy tales, however alluring they may seem now, were hollow compared to my experiences journeying to the other world. The space of dreaming and dreams is more real than anyone can imagine.

A density and strength runs through my experience, which will never go away or be shattered by harsh reality. If the dreams are real, I think to myself, then how can they not affect us in body, just as if we are together in flesh, exchanging the atoms of our energy? And if our collective dreaming makes such profound healing possible and works in such untold ways, then my Goddess, what about all relationships and situations of my life? The possibilities are endless – healing, creating, changing destiny, past life traumas dissipated. Now I am truly floored. Because I realize -- finally -- that my life and the way I lead it will never be ordinary again.

Sugar & Spice

Inexpression

(For David Rich)

I

Voice quivers, recognition
Greetings whisked down gullies
Over rivers, canyons
Swirling Atlantic tidal flow

Demands words together
Dandelion meadows
Offerings, symbolic cushions
Delayed arrivals

Like dreams –
Flowing eternal rhythm
Boxes with stories
Airborne viewpoints

Like bird's gliding visions

(Dream)

Church's dark pews
Stretch empty waiting
Priest's holy words reverberating
Incense burns –

Memory's dying embers
Musty cellars, lichen walls
Pale pastel wedding suits
Tight collars

II

Floating footsteps
Grey haze
Sideways glance
Mouth not speaking

Eyes hidden in shadow
Pierce like swords
Into my soul

III

Your shape –
Tails and top hat –
Ducks archway to light
Green, muddy grass

Seeping through white
Vows under tree
Multitudes of summer hats
Sinking heels

Blue sky, puffy clouds
Saints statues surrounded
By bushes,
I lose you

Ducks archway to light
Green, muddy grass

Seeping through white
Vows under tree
Multitudes of summer hats
Sinking heels

Blue sky, puffy clouds
Saints statues surrounded
By bushes,
I lose you

IV

Return inside to solitude
Shiny shoes hard-soled
On cold stone
Jarring me ahead

Search among pews
Dust stuck in my throat
Shoulder blades oppressed
Shadows flickering on walls

V

She looks at me
Up the aisle
Tiny hat askew
Ribbons down back

Gloved hands, perfect lips
Eyes innocent questions
Wise, round face, dimple
Her flower petals

Soft and warm
Dropped to floor
Sweetly scented
I lay them in her
Wicker basket

VI

You appear black
Against overexposed light
Kneel beside me
Hand brushes wrist

Feel blood flow
Hat brim obscures
Eyes shining blue
Your head dips

To kiss my lips
Dream ends –
Feelings left unsaid…

(Epilogue)

Voice lingers
Waits for meanings –

Pies cooling
Castles view
Sheltered island cove

Sadness overwhelms expectation
Twisted meetings on the edge
While moments last

What does it mean –
The beach's dark ocean,
Istanbul's lights dancing
Alone, wind in my hair
You arrive speaking
In terry cloth robes?

May 1995

The Mouse

The mouse across the room
Squeaks
Jabbing tones and cadences
Irritating my inner ear

Her complaining, squawky voice
Blaming
Capturing the room her sound echoes
Irritating my whole body

The mouse across the room
Finally lets another speak
Oh beautiful silence!
Left without annoying chatter

Irritating my whole rhythm

1994

Haiku #1

Seasons of growing
Like brown leaves falling are the
Wisdom of knowing

1994

Out in Left Field

Somewhere floating in the clouds
I meet my understanding

The cottony fluff –
Mind's uncharted ribbons

Speaking to the nebulous
Out in left field

We become lost connections
Space between eternities

Linger waiting
Opportunity's fallen victim

Asking:
What shall I do when I get there?

Answering, as you do,
With a joke – some forlorn analogy

II

I see darkness
Ponder the twisting of the moon

Under your gaze
Crackle of twirling leaves

Wind's harsh howling
While the clock hits morning

Yet to discover lilacs blooming
Or feel the warmth from your
fingertips

In chilly morning dew
Space between existence

Only –
I know you.

Circa 2003

Shrouded in Mystery

Kilburn

(Days)

Snaking Victorians,
Varied states of repair
Dog surprise,
Chocolate wrapper
Un-swept pink petals

Haggard ladies
Languid babies dribble salty crisps
Overwhelming Persil boxes
Sway against stroller wheels

Mangy stray dogs –
Fur matted, claws clicking
Dodge trees and feet
Glistening noses sniff turds

Car exhaust puffs
Acrid, asthma inducing diesel
Leaded kids laugh,
Noses wet with snot

Kilburn market –
Fruit and veg, red nylon teddies
Platform shoes
Cheap and sordid
From dirty grab barrels
Buck-toothed underwear lady
And Irish crooners

(Nights)

Pub window's light
Red-nosed locals
Overflowing Guinness,
Whiskey shorts
19th Century woodwork ceilings

Irish jigs
Folk, Jazz, Blues
Rave's rhythmic booming
Jovial laughs,
Stout drinkers' incoherent singing

Greek kebab houses
Compressed, greasy meat
With salad
Chippies and Burger King
Late night marts

Sick looking,
Disheveled patrons
Waiting for night buses
Snogging couples

Screams,
Jeering catcalls
Drunken meandering
Slurs for spare change
Greetings –

"You 'ave nice legs…"
"You American?"
"What ya doin' in Kilburn?"

June 1995

Joe's Drums

Somewhere deep inside my covers it feels safe and he is here. I can feel his strong arms and the warmth of his breath on my cheek. Joe with his tangled complicated self all wrapped up around me in a good place where we try not to merge too fast or to merge at all. Building trust. Some would say we trust too much about some things and not enough about others.

I wonder where Joe's physical body is, just for a moment but I am keenly aware of where his spirit resides right now as I lay resting in my bed and so it doesn't matter too much to me where he is in body. He whispers all his dreams in my ear and I listen, through my heart. That place where we meet, however briefly is the place where my soul melts into his and we are more than we'll ever be alone.

Writing about these things comes with difficulty because the feelings are so ethereal. Sometimes I find my mind wondering and imagining another place in time. A moment in my life when I asked God, "Who is this man anyway?" The uncanny familiarity that spoke to the knowing of each other from another life coupled with the insecurity of not knowing each other at all in this one is palpable and real.

"I don't even know what he wants from a relationship!" I plead with Spirit.

Spirit answers, "Just run to him and love him with everything you have. There are no consequences except what happens when you are not loving."

I see myself treading water in this really murky swamp. My position dangerous and powerful at the same time because my heart flies from my chest, no longer bound by the conventions of protecting the pumping, emotional, fickle, necessary organ from the pain that comes from breaking. In fact, I cannot hold back even if I want to, not without feeling the emptiness -- barren of possibility and devoid of creative essence -- that comes from not bringing my entire soul to the situation.

This type of danger thrills me; catapulting, stretching, throwing and exploding my essence into teeny-tiny shards. I am hoping beyond hope that somehow the eventual contraction will put it all back together again – maybe in different places and with new facets yet to be uncovered. Despite how it feels, the experience of knowing Joe is not draining at all even though at times I re-live the worst of the draining aspects of my past relationships. Maybe those memories come up, like gushing pustules, just so I can see them again, acknowledge the learning those moments gave me and simply be given the opportunity to let them go? With answers like these, there are always more questions.

I am with Joe and he touches me in some deep part of myself awakening the deepest sense of feeling inside my being. It is like I am somewhere floating in the stars up there in space, no longer weighed down by the heaviness of this body I inhabit day-by-day.

I can remember his caress, the one where I feel like I am being played like one of his instruments. In that moment, he's got one of his drumsticks in his hand or a guitar with the strings all taut and well-tuned. He's a master of the music. It's flowing through him without remorse, full of feeling and he is doing what he was born to this earth to do – listen to the tunes of the heavens and interpret them for the rest of us.

His grip on this instrument of mine is strong and secure and he is playing it and finding all the right notes. I can feel the melody welling up inside, slowly splitting the atoms of my spirit into pieces -- strings, drums, brass and then the harmony voice joining in completion. The rhythm of Joe's fingers playing with my hair and slowly running over my skin has an intoxicating quality, which truly amazes me and brings me to my knees. The whole dynamic is big and cacophonous. What he is reaches in and holds my soul for just a minute, directing the piece he plays with a

gentleness belying his absolute talent and in that moment I see the whole Universe.

In a burst of light, I experience how I fit into the cosmic order like a heavenly piece of energy that is whole and individual at the same time. I feel my complex uniqueness and the power of my oneness in that exact nanosecond when the warmth emanating from the pads of his soft fingers touches the coolness of my jawbone. Sparks fly through every cell of my being. The Universe is bigger and brighter than I could have ever imagined and I fit there. I am not on the outside anymore. I am required and needed like nothing has ever been needed before. As valued as any other part of the Universe where everything has its place and if I were not in this exact position the Universe just would not function. There would be a clicking and a popping and a dissonance rather than the beautiful sound that Joe makes playing the notes from my strings.

I feel, while I am in his presence, this man gains great pleasure in the art of what he does from that place of pure knowing. He has infinite understanding from playing the instrument he finds within me and yet he is amazed that he has discovered it at all.

"Am I really that talented?" he asks God.

Spirit says, "Joe, you are the musician, we gave you the gift of playing love for others to hear, why would you doubt the gift we gave you? You touch others, and in the moment that you do they feel me and know I love them more than life itself."

Joe cries out in that encounter and lets go. Afraid that spirit might require of him more than he knows how to give.

I sense the momentary hesitation caused by Joe's confusion, he misses a beat within me and at once I am taken from that place of love and harmony. The room grows cold and my spine shivers. The Universe of stars receeds from view. My heart skips a beat and I am forced to suck in air and let it out slowly, grappling to regain my composition. I see it all when he plays those notes within me and my tears fall hot down my cheeks from the emptiness that comes from missing. And yet he loves his music too much to let it go completely.

He's shattered just the same, head-in-hand; he allows the drumstick to fall clattering on the floor from the weakness of his grip. He looks down upon the creamy wood, one eye hidden behind his hand and the other a blinking, gray pool of anguish. Remembering the moment in vivid realism when someone somewhere told him he wasn't good enough and branding Joe with the concept that being a musician was less than God's expectation because in reality no one survives on love alone.

Joe is hostile now and churning. He turns the power of his love in on himself wishing only to beat a rhythm from his bones as deafening as the rage that comes from being turned from the only thing he knows how to do. Believing that this talent is only a curse while the rest of his life leaves him behind.

I take his hand in mine; my tears fall from my chin and splash onto his fingers. With the other hand, I pick up his stick, fingering the grains of wood, still warm from where he held it in his palm. I play with his fingers, running mine up and down his knuckles, over his palm. Massaging the calluses and getting to know every aspect of his hands so I that I can remember them. He watches me do this. I want to tell him what it is like to be played by him and how my life will never be the same, knowing that he can show me love in a way that no one else has ever been able to do. A love, deeper and stronger than any words or actions on the physical plane.

There is nothing mortal about what I feel. His voice is vibrant, grander and more universal than trite words alone. And I think when he plays the notes he derives equal pleasure from the sound the notes make to him – the beautiful music. Maybe that is what the guides mean when they say:

"He is writing a song for you."

Maybe they mean he is writing the song and playing it within me? He learns my range and the quality of the sound I produce. He understands what combinations of harmonics and melodies are possible. Any literal song he is writ-

ing pales in comparison to the one he writes when he touches me because it is in that space that the real poetry of the Universe spills forth.

I feel the words and the music well up inside me each time I am with Joe. I feel myself singing to him sometimes – like the siren song of the whales, that lovely and haunting tune that tells the stories of their history and all the love that comes from their large hearts. There is intelligence in those moments that no words can describe. I almost feel as if I touch God. Joe touches spirit and brings it forth inside my body.

I wonder, "What do I do for you Joe?"

Is the hearing of my song equally as important as the playing of it is to me?

I place the drumstick back into his palm and close his fingers around it once again. I look into his deep gray eyes and send all the love I have in my heart out to him, holding him and caressing his soul. Poor, gentle Joe. The one who knows how to play my song but cannot yet find his own. He uses his busyness to reflect all the attention. He defends his position rather than celebrating his life. All the parental phone calls represent for him the destruction of his essence and yet upon hearing that all God wants is for him to play his drums for the world, he runs from the voice of spirit within him. Kicking and screaming, he thinks that what he has just experienced is yet another damming phone call telling him to find something productive to do with this existence.

In this place between dreaming and awake, I can recall a LeAnn Rimes song. I start singing it clearly and passionately, sending the sentiment forth for Joe to catch with his fist somewhere, wherever he is right now. The fiddle and the quiet drum. A little steel guitar and some keyboards create the melody.

"God only knows how I've needed a friend/ Who can see the boldness and pride/ Someone strong enough I can put my faith in/ Someone willing to let me inside. So be a man/And be my man."

The chorus wells and overflows, spilling the contents of my aching heart into the cup of creative space:

"I dare you to need me like nobody else…Kiss me/ Leave the world standing still...I dare you to want to want/ To wanna be good to me."

The song ends and I am left quiet inside. I sigh.

The day is bright and hot. I am walking up the hill near Joe's house. Joe pulls up beside me in his silver car and turns down the music. I can feel the sweat dripping down my back; the rayon shirt I am wearing is stifling and uncomfortable. I know what he is going to say even before he says it and I am self-conscious. My voice is stuck in my throat and my hand shakes.

I cry out to God, "What else does he need?"

Spirit answers, "It isn't what he needs that matters today, it is what you need."

Joe speaks to me and his lips are moving; I can barely hear him over the din. My strings break one by one. I can hear them pinging and feel them curling, snapping back from their bolts and slapping me in the face. He can't see the truth but the welts swell and seep. He tells me that this relationship is only casual and his serious energy is devoted to his career. I want to tell him that in my experience there is nothing casual about him. There is only the deep longing that comes from knowing he knows how to play me and won't anymore.

I can't look at him. My poetry gets mangled and garbled by the heavy hum that vibrates over our conversation. He's not speaking to God and spirit's voice is silent. I can't pretend that what he offers is enough for me, not after having the tune, the beautiful music. How can I accept the silence?

I walk away from him, down the hill. Having said things I didn't mean. Sadness permeates my being just as the

spring jasmine scents the gardens I walk past.

"God, I hurt. You didn't tell me it would hurt to awaken my song."

Spirit answers, "What hurts is not the awakening but the choice Joe made in walking away from his instrument. Sometimes loving someone means letting them go and yet, loving is always a good thing."

I picture Joe at his drum set. He's looking down at his hands and feeling the sticks. There's a song in there somewhere but he wonders why he doesn't want to play today. I am listening to his breath and seeing his chest rise and fall in quiet acquiescence. There is tension in his jaw. I can watch him just fine from where I am. His strong, broad shoulders as he sits on his stool; I remember the feel of his arms. His painting he was working on and once showed me is finished and sits on the easel by the workbench. I come behind him and caress his shoulders. Drawing my hand over his skin. Massaging his neck.

I whisper in Joe's ear, "It's OK baby, you have everything you need to play your song."

Joe looks around, wondering if he heard his name. No one appears at the garage door. He's not looking in the right place to see me.

Joe speaks to God, "Don't you understand? All my energy is spent trying to make it work. Everyone just wants to take all the time -- take my desire, ask me to be less, prostitute myself for the sake of fitting in. I am harassed. I am told I am crazy. God, I feel crazy sometimes, ya know? What kind of peace is there? What kind of time is there to devote to love?"

Spirit answers, "The only kind of time you have, Joe. The time of your life. What else is there but love? When you have the instrument in front of you. You know how to play and the song comes from me through you. If you refuse to play the song I send you because you are afraid then what's the point of having the instrument? Whether it is the woman or your drums. The song is stifled in your heart. You choke it. You spit in the face of the beautiful gifts that are given to you. Fear of not being enough, Joe, is the only thing that holds you back from everything you desire."

"But God, what about all the work it takes to make it in the business? To get that job in the studio and to create the film score? The money I don't have to cut an album. There's no time!"

Joe's tears fall steadily down his cheeks. The phone rings on the bench. Joe's Dad wanting to know if he got that good paying job they talked about last week; Joe lets it go to voicemail.

"See what I mean, God?"

Joe's voice catches just a little. He gets angry because he hears laughter. He forgets that God's laughter is not about making fun but about the love She has for Joe, a love so immense, there's no end to patience and joy. Joe's just a wonderful, creative soul who needs Her protection and love.

"There's no work in the creative life Joe, you make it hard work because you feel that God wouldn't give you anything without asking a price for it. Your Dad loves you very much but he thinks life is supposed to be a certain way with clearly defined limits. He forgets that God wants inspiration to flow like a river of gold, steady and true and that God's only compensation is the beautiful music you play. Your gift is beyond time, beyond words. You play your drums. You play the woman who loves you and she spills forth the bounty of her own creative juices. That is all I ask of you."

I watch and listen. I want to appear to Joe. Walk up the driveway and knock on the garage door. That's the way it works in the movies. I'll make that movie one day and it will have the happy ending. My own children screeching around my kitchen, the pots brimming with good smells and the living room filled with friends. My children are laughing gleefully around me -- whole, dynamic, wonderful creative souls. Maybe one will be a drummer, like Joe.

My life is at once filled with the possibilities. These thoughts expand out in the infinite boom of the explosion created by the synergy that comes from knowing where I am headed. I skip down the sidewalk wearing the orange

dress that fits me like a glove. The lights of downtown blink and the night air is warm and pregnant. Summer's coming and my life is exactly where I need it to be.

I walk around in the dark, listening to the harmony within that I know how to find now and thinking of Joe. My body dances to the rhythm of my own beat. I walk past the restaurant where he plays some nights. I see him there in the candlelight. He's got a drink in his hands and he's looking straight at me. I laugh. He did always know how to find me, ever since I met him that first night -- he saw me enter the room and followed me with his eyes long before I knew he was interested. He's wearing that same shirt he wore when we met. I can remember the feel of it against my cheek. I can smell him again -- that clean smell augmented with some woodsy cologne.

I wave. He waves back. In that instant, I know everything is going to be OK. Somehow, it will work out. There's no song but the song we play for each other. He couldn't lose me even if he tried. I dare him in my mind, as I head back to my car. I dare him to play his song, louder, stronger, and bigger than he ever thought possible. I know he can. That drumstick is one with his hand.

Spirit says, "There's no question but the one you answer with your heart. Joe may not see it now but there's love bigger than the both of you, if only you ask it of me. The talent you already have; you were born with the knowing. The love is flowing from your heart; you speak his name and he hears you. Sometimes you have to be patient to get what you desire the most. There's no work involved when you flow with my voice inside you and speak your truth. Only good can come from this."

I smile. The warmth of God's love grows in my solar plexus like a sun emanating a great heat. Joe plays his drums. I speak my words. I am the poet; he's the musician. I write the song and he plays the tune. And wherever we are, we know how to find each other. There's no trick. There's no work or struggle. I know he's walking somewhere in the wooded hills. Smelling the green and pungent scents of spring. He's remembering that time we kissed under a tree with the light filtering gently through the leaves. He's bouncing from rock to rock and singing a blues tune. Something old. Something on vinyl.

I dance. I dare him. I speak Joe'a name and he turns his head trying to see if he can locate where I am. He knows how to find me in the crowd even if I pretend to hide from him. I finish the film so he can write the score. We love each other beyond the borders of convention and other people's ideas of what is right.

I ask God, "So what's next?"

Spirit answers, "The man who let's you win his heart."

I laugh, allowing the sounds to shake my body from head to toe and knowing the man God is speaking of is somewhere close by and he's already listening to my song.

Into the Music of Life

Soul Brother

Dark smoky tombs
Your eyes dance
Unable to grasp
Reality shifts

Faster
Harder
You berate me
For not being

What you know I am --
Sorceress
Priestess of the maiden moon
Third eye seer

II

I know you
Spirit man
Soul brother
Love

You say I'll never know
Deep dark secret keeper
In the light of the night
I whisper:

"Tell me..."
Light body
Higher self same man
Speaks the truth without you
knowing

Pure hatred
Rape
Drumstick sadness
Lingers

Like oil in the oceans
Dark and seeping
Story reveals
Time now to let it go

III

Your soul sings
Cries to be free
Torture mingles
Tears spread your flesh apart

Searing
Hot poker
Fucker
And they didn't believe you did they?

Fearful
Tearful
Fighting words bubble
Cascade

Froth at the mouth
Terrible disdain
You scream:
"Tell me how to get there – you know the way!"

Thing is…I can't
The path is yours to take
Wolf stealer
Medicine drummer

Take your feather headdress
Your gourd rattle
Restore
Rescue

Your own soul
From the ashes of despair
Retrieve the wisdom
Gauntlet sucker

IV

Your malevolent empress
Uses her sword
Cutting the bullshit
In pieces

Down to the core
Smell the blood
Nothing to hide behind
You run

Scared
And yet you run no further
Truth teller
I know

I lied
I know
The deeper
Darker spiritual secret you keep ---

Hollow
Drunken
Stoner poetry
When the words

“I love you”
Cast light upon the shadow
Of self-loathing
And finally

Frantically
You begin to heal.

May 15, 2005

The Water Dragon
(one of the four elementals)

The Musician

Sultry lights
Mirrored reflection
Quiet rumbling

Conversation pumping
Red wine glass
Grilled shrimp tasty

Shared festive
Company
Delightful squishy bread

Jazz tunes
Harmony
Cascading

Somber notes
Reminds me
Tempered jungle drumming

Deep circadian rhythms

II

I see you
Filtering the beat
Red-hot cinnamon walls

Candlelight
Staccato profile
I know you

Watch every move
We meet in a space
Deeper than one life

Like we know Christmas
Warm and cozy
I feel you

Humming
Forever –
From the outside looking in

III

Emotional turmoil
Ships passing in the night
Heart struggles

Painful seeking
No one's walls
Another lifetime

Always love
Why did it have to be you?

IV

You saw him
Deep inside your beat
Leaving

Like we never met
Running
Faster than my heart

Darkened
Rainy
Moonless night

Blinking foggy stars
Universal jolting
Passing the scene

Never returning
You take me
Floating

Panting
Past despair
Into the light

March 11, 2005

Him

He lies sleeping
Peacefully whispering
Baby eyes
The man of my dreams

Not

Only a man
Warm embrace
Soft petal kisses

Needs harder than the world
Larger than life's dreams
Excavated talent
Stop thinking

Voices
Ringing

Be

February 2, 2005

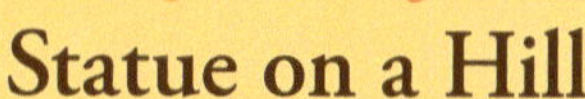

Statue on a Hill

Made once on farmer's land
I stand tall and proud
Towering over rolling green hills

Wherever you might come
You see me
Set behind the trees

Arms extending outward
Beckoning from afar
My eyes see before me

People come for miles
Guests and hidden baggage
They may come to learn

To Escape
Always leaving changed
Rain soaked hills

Millennia marching on
The farmer loved,
His family owned my feet

He looked to where I stand
Seeing far beyond me
Now you come to find

Gray rainy day distasteful
Water gushes rivulets
Around my ankles

Swims through my fingers
Pours through my hair
My eyes shaded from sight

I am forever cold.
You come to ask me questions
I find a way to keep you warm

I answer your thoughts
Maybe you will find --
The seeking always do.

Circa 1994

Wolf Stealer's Heart

I

Joanie watched surreptitiously as her grandfather opened the package, the one wrapped in brown paper that she had signed for up at the big house and then brought down to him in his studio. The package, stamped "Special Delivery" and "Handle with Care," arrived on the early morning delivery with an air of mystery, and she was going to get to the bottom of what it contained. In Joanie's hand, was one of the books on her summer reading list, a mystery series with her favorite character, "Casey Doolittle, Teenage Sleuth: Mystery of the Broken Mirror."

Joanie sat on the comfy brown leather sofa, with her grandmother's hand-crocheted chunky green afghan wrapped around her like a cocoon; she pretended to read her book, while keeping one eye on Grandfather. Grandfather was being awfully methodical and Joanie got antsy. After he placed the package on the dining table, she observed him studying the outside of the brown paper packaging, carefully removing the tape and unfolding the paper, sliding the paper off the enclosed item and folding the paper slowly, as though he were saving it for something important. Joanie rolled her eyes and tried to find the paragraph she had been reading in her book earlier that morning.

Joanie's grandfather shifted slightly and she looked up from the page just in case she could catch a glimpse of what he was doing but his back blocked her view. Frustrated, she cleared her throat, hoping he would turn around and at least say something but to no avail; he was apparently lost in thought. Sighing, she took in her surroundings instead. The photos and memorabilia on the wall from her grandfather's career, his award case filled with gold statuettes and glass plaques. His drum and tambourine collection, especially the one given to him by the Native American healer decorated with Eagle feathers; she liked the way the drum sounded when her grandfather played. Her hand slid over the soft, worn leather sofa and she breathed in, deeply. She loved the smell of the old leather.

Sometimes she thought about all the stories this piece of furniture could tell. Grandfather's friends came in all shapes and sizes, after all and most of them were well-known musicians. She chuckled to herself when she pictured how the sofa sure had seen a lot of famous butts! Grandfather looked over at the sound of Joanie's giggle with that inquisitive look of his, his steely grey-blue eyes cutting through to the middle of her soul, like he read her mind.

She knew he could -- see through her, into her. There was that time he visited her in New York when her family still lived there. She was seven or eight. She stole candy from the convenience store while her grandfather was busy at the magazine rack. He gave her that same deep look and no sooner had the cashier rung up the magazine, her grandfather asked Joanie if she would like to pay for the candy in her pocket. Joanie, mortified and embarrassed beyond belief had simply put the candy bar back on the shelf and said nothing.

Joanie's eyes quickly darted back to her book, her heart racing. Where was that paragraph now? To her surprise, Joanie's grandfather came and sat next to her on the sofa. He let out a big sigh and reached over to take her hand in his. They sat there in silence, Grandfather's big, rough, warm hand surrounding her smaller one. She wondered if she had done something wrong or if he had something bad to say? She was not exactly sure what to do next.

Joanie's mind gravitated through flashbacks of the last week since Grandfather received that mysterious phone call. She had been sitting on this very same sofa, talking about her riding lesson and how Whiptail, her favorite pony, had stumbled and she being thrown, had fallen into a big steaming pile of horse poop (so gross!) and how she narrowly missed landing face-down. Joanie's grandfather -- usually attentive to her stories of catastrophe and the important details regarding her friends from prep school -- had taken a phone call and, instead of saying he would call back when he was out of the business meeting like he usually did, he cut her story short with a big hand gesture. Within minutes, he put his hand on the receiver and asked Joanie to go back to the big house; he needed

to be alone for awhile.

Unaccustomed to being blown off, she had cried all the way back home and slammed the front door on her way in, causing her mother to look up from the manuscript she had been editing in the study, a room located to the right of the entry foyer. She heard her mother say something garbled about taking more care, which she ignored, and spent the rest of the afternoon locked in her room playing the interactive sleuth-inspired game "Mystery Hunt," with her friends on the Net. What the hell was wrong with her grandfather anyway?

The fact was, since Joanie and her family had moved into the big house after the death of her grandmother, Sarah, and Grandfather had moved permanently into his studio, he had always made time for Joanie. Joanie's Mom said they were moving so that they could all take care of each other and Joanie made sure to visit her grandfather often and keep an eye on him and his music buddies. The old guys liked to sit around the studio and talk of the past and laugh about the things they used to get up to and occasionally, they would have a jam session that would put some of the younger bands her friends prefered, to shame.

While it was true that Joanie's grandfather was normally a little peculiar, he had been downright mysterious since receiving "The Call," as everyone at home now termed the phone conversation, in which, as she later found out, Grandfather was notified that an old friend of his had passed away. Locking himself in his studio for hours on end, drumming while avoiding her and the rest of the family was clearly not his usual modus operandi. He had been at it for days afterward, neither coming to the big house nor answering his phone and he had gotten everyone worried. Music played in Grandfather's house nearly 24-hours a day, the old records like Bob Marley and Sadé. Joanie's grandfather still played the vinyl stuff that no one else in the world owned anymore on his beat up record player. But all day drumming -- this was completely over-the-top even for him!

Joanie's Mom finally wormed her way into the studio after a few days, but upon returning would say nothing to her about what happened in their conversation, only that Grandfather needed his privacy at this time. Joanie's Mom in an effort to make her feel better did show her the location of the family scrapbooks made by Grandma Sarah of years past when Grandfather played his jazz drums at the big concert halls in Europe and clubs in New York. He had even appeared on TV a few times and went to the Oscars during those days when the films he scored came out in theaters.

She was even able to see pictures of Grandfather's friend, the one who had just died, a pretty woman with brown hair. The woman made films and had several books published according to the journaling. She was often seen in the pictures of their family travels around the world in groupings of unusual looking medicine men with tattoos and feathers in their hair or near animals, like elephants in the African safari, smiling as though she was having the time of her life. In one of the pictures, Grandfather was receiving his medicine drum; the one Joanie liked so much. The caption read: "Benjamin is given the medicine drum by Chief Red Hawk at the Tribal Nations Pow Wow.

In another picture, the aforementioned woman was shown with her arm around a small child, the caption read: "The Empress with Nambi, the orphan at the hospital in Kenya." There was also another line of text next to the photo, "The Empress' husband was down with a bad case of dysentery this trip and is therefore in none of these pictures. We joked that night that she was looking awfully single and that the press might pick up on this later and make up fantastic stories about the demise of her once great marriage. Sadly, this all ended up to be true!...see next page." Joanie turned the page to see a yellowed copy of the front page of the National Enquirer with a harried looking woman, barely recognizable as her grandfather's friend and the headline, "The Empress fails the test. Her marriage dissolves in shambles over the desire to adopt orphan Kenyan girl." Joanie chuckled.

Joanie's grandmother had made these albums of all their travels; her Grandfather's career highlights and special family events. She included written journals of who was in the pictures, the story behind events and newspaper clippings, train tickets, you name it. She had been really into the history of the family and it was great to be able to read through those old stories, like the time Grandfather was really late for a big gig in New York and left his stick bag on the train. He had arrived at his destination in time to do a quick sound check with the band only to discover the missing bag. His assistant was calling the train company and he was ducking into the audience to search for

musicians who might have drumsticks in their car - he found one finally in the ninth row and later gave the guy a bottle of champagne and free tickets to his next gig in New York for his trouble.

In the following days, Joanie poured over these albums of her grandfather's life, which kept her occupied enough that the worry she felt for his well-being was at least subdued with the interest of learning more about the history of the family. She was especially keen on learning more about the relationship he had with his long-time business partner who had so recently passed away. She looked like such a fantastic person, the kind of woman you would spend time shopping with or horse-back riding with and really look up to, not someone who was boring at all. The doors to the studio, however, remained locked and Grandfather's incessant drumming emanated from the building like an eerie ghost of death and dying, a mournful cadence of the sadness in her Grandfather's heart.

Then finally the situation changed. A package arrived in the mail for Joanie's grandfather. Her mother told her to take it down to the studio because Grandfather expected the item. She had looked forward to finally getting to see him again and maybe just maybe they could watch his old films again, like they used to. She would make popcorn and he would tell her stories of all the stuff that happened in production, like how the lead actor's on set extramarital tryst with the woman playing his college-age daughter halted production for two weeks while they dealt with the media storm. He would be back to his old self.

Now that she was sitting on the brown leather couch in silence while her grandfather sat there stupefied she realized he was more mysterious and less like his old self than ever. Just as if he read her mind, Joanie's grandfather got up, went to the table and brought back the framed picture. On closer inspection, it turned out to be a drawing, which Joanie realized was of two fairies; she knew this because both of them had wings with glitter. Grandfather ran his calloused hand over the girl fairy's face, leaving a smudge on the glass. His eyes got a little watery but he tried to cover it up by pretending to sneeze and dabbing at his eyes with a tissue. Joanie rolled her eyes at her grandfather and took the opportunity to take a good look at the drawing. What she saw were two fairies in what looked like one of those jazz clubs Grandfather used to play in more often than he did now.

These clubs were always a bit dark inside with little lamps on the tables and waitresses who would bring her Coke with cherries in it just like she was an adult. She had been a little girl around eight the last time she was at one of these clubs and she knew that the only reason she was allowed there was because her grandfather was headlining. They were often noisy until the music started and then everyone was quiet as a mouse, all eyes on her grandfather and the other guys in the band.

The guy fairy had drumsticks in his hands. How funny? Just like Grandfather. Joanie recognized the cymbal and the snare drum. The girl fairy had a magic wand with a star on the top. They seemed to be laughing with each other about something only the two of them knew about. The drumstick and the wand were touching. The girl fairy's wand had hearts coming from it and the guy's had music notes. What was all that about? In the background was a table. And what was that stuff? A wolf's head? A couple of other objects she did not recognize. What a weird scene!

Then her eyes scanned over to the sign hanging from the tree in the picture. The sign read: "Woodland Jazz Club." And then underneath that, "Playing Tonight" with a name written there that looked a lot like Grandfather's except it was spelled funny. That was strange. Joanie looked over at her grandfather who was sitting next her staring off into space and occasionally dabbing his eyes with a tissue.

Realizing that she was watching him he said, "Girl, these allergies are just getting bad with me these days. Don't get old. All you do is fall apart."

Joanie knew her grandfather did not have allergies but she let him think that she believed him anyway.

"Grandfather," she asked, "what's with the wolf head and all that stuff on the table? And who is Benjawood Mullerberry? That sounds like your name kinda, doesn't it?"

"Ha," Grandfather exclaimed! He looked over the drawing as if seeing it for the first time. Joanie had a funny feeling Grandfather had seen this picture a few times before. "Well, in order to understand why there is a wolf head I'd have to tell you the story of Wolf Stealer." Joanie was waiting for him to go on but he was busy blowing his nose.

"Who is Wolf Stealer? So I am right, that is a wolf head on the table and what are those other objects? Now that I look closer one seems to look like that little medicine drum you gave me for my birthday. Is that what it is?" Joanie asked all at once.

Her grandfather took a deep breath. "Girl, you ask a lot of questions."

"Well you've been weird for over a week and now you get this drawing of a couple of fairies. And well, I think you are being very mysterious, if you ask me." Joanie added emphatically.

Joanie's Grandfather looked down at her but still did not say anything right away, which was very frustrating to Joanie. Joanie did not remember Grandfather's business partner in person; she only knew her from the scrapbooks. Joanie's Mom did say that The Empress, as a lot of people called her, used to come to family gatherings many years ago and had also travelled with the family when Joanie's Mom was a kid. Still, she had obviously been a super important part of Grandfather's life if he was this upset. What was all the fuss about anyway? Maybe they had an affair? In which case, why was Grandma Sarah so nice to her? Joanie knew there were answers she wasn't getting, after all Casey Doolittle always suspected the people who didn't say anything more than the people who said too much.

"So you want to hear the story of Wolf Stealer huh?" Joanie's grandfather interrupted her investigatory thoughts.

Joanie nodded her head, thinking to herself that any storytelling would be better than the sullen, quiet and aloof grandfather she had been accustomed to lately.

"Well, you better get comfortable, it's a long one," Grandfather added.

Joanie flashed her grandfather one of her signature smiles and he gave her a wink. At least a few things were getting back to normal. She got comfortable on the couch, with her feet on his lap, as they always did when conversing and waited for Grandfather to begin his story.

"This story takes place a long, long time ago in an Ojibwa Indian village that was located near what is now known as the Great Lakes in the State of Wisconsin...," Joanie's grandfather began the story.

II

In the Ojibwa village lived a great shaman priest named Wolf Stealer. He was called Wolf Stealer because when he was a young boy, almost ready to be named a man; he went on his Guardian Spirit Quest, a sort of journey that all young men and women of the tribe took where they traveled into the wilderness to learn their totem animal and initiate into adulthood. The quest led him to the mouth of a wolf den. His spirit guides showed him the way in a vision to enter the den undetected by covering himself in the droppings of the wolf.

Once his eyes adjusted to the dimness of the den he witnessed a great sight, a female wolf tending to her young. That night, he slept on pine needles nestled amongst the nearby trees and when the dawn came he went back to the mouth of the wolf den. Covering himself again in the droppings, he slipped into the den without raising awareness, just as he had the evening before.

He carefully removed one of the cubs, a female cub he later name Sheba. He gave thanks to the Great Spirit for this gift, making an offering in exchange and performing a dance in Spirit's honor. Sheba grew to be a great she-

wolf, a totem animal for the village -- protector of the shaman and a profound symbol for the people of Wolf Stealer's tribe who made their home in the forests near and around the Great Lakes. The tribe was a happy one.

Comprised of talented warriors, storytellers and hunters, this small tribe grew prosperous from the trading they did with neighboring tribes and later with the white man. The tribe made their home by the seasons, moving from place to place as the weather and hunting required.

The great Warrior Chief who was wise and strong ruled the tribe and at his right hand was the shaman priest who was said to hold the soul of the tribe in the palm of his hand. Wolf Stealer became a powerful priest, one who came from a long line of shamans called by the Great Spirit and initiated by the Chief of the Sky Spirits during his Guardian Spirit Quest. Women, warriors and children all came to him in times of illness or for his advice in matters of importance or simply to tell him of a dream they had which they thought might be pertinent to the tribe.

In his healing work, Wolf Stealer would go into deep trances using his ankle rattles and medicine drum to create a beat and rhythm while at the same time humming and toning with his voice. His journeying to the Underworld while in trance brought the soul of his brother or sister back from the land of Spirits where they were lost. In these times, the whole village depended on Wolf Stealer and his talents to keep illness and disease from spreading. Disease, Wolf Stealer knew from experience and training, came from disquiet in the heart, a heart he held in his own soul. A heart he could feel beating when he slept, distinct from the beating of his own heart and yet inside him nevertheless.

Sheba, whom he had hand-raised, was always by his side, a steady companion. There were times when Wolf Stealer stayed in the Underworld for several days doing his healing work and it was then that Sheba would hunt for him, bring back a rabbit or small rodent so that when he awoke, tired and hungry, the women of the village would already have cleaned and cooked his meal.

Wolf Stealer knew herbs as well. He would frequently take a woman with him while he searched for the herbs in the forests around the village. She would carry them in her basket, freeing him to search under rocks, climb steep areas and dig under tree roots to find that for which he searched. It was on one of these expeditions, that Wolf Stealer met a hunting group traveling from another tribe. One member of the party was injured, a young warrior, who had fallen and broken his leg while showing off his climbing skill. Far from their tribe and shaman, the hunting group was fearful they would lose this young man to the Spirit World.

Meeting Wolf Stealer by chance in the woods, they were overjoyed to notice the mark of the Shaman and so offered the young woman traveling with them as a bride in exchange for Wolf Stealer's healing work. At first, Wolf Stealer waved them away not wishing to be encumbered by another woman on his journey back to his tribe. While he worked his healing magic, however, the young woman was his constant companion -- cutting and cooking herbs, gathering wood for the fire and making his meals. Her brother was the young warrior lying ill and she wished very much to see his return to the Earth and for him to be healthy once again.

A feeling grew in Wolf Stealer's heart as he watched the woman tend so carefully for her brother and work so diligently on his behalf. And so it was that by the time the young man was well enough to be transported back home, Wolf Stealer took Sings Like Rain as his wife and together with her new tribe sister, they walked back to the village to meet the Warrior Chief and other members of the family.

Like her name suggested, Sings Like Rain's voice reminded Wolf Stealer of the summer rain, melodic and sweet. She would often sing as she did her work and sometimes would catch Wolf Stealer staring at her, as he liked to do. When she did notice him watching her, she would smile and a great warmth leapt in his heart for he had grown to love Sings Like Rain very deeply. She transitioned easily into the tribe even though she still missed her brother and mother who she knew she might never see again. She worked well with the other women sowing corn, squash, and pumpkin, cooking meals, preparing meat and making baskets. She was also very adept at berry gathering and Wolf Stealer was able to teach her about the herb lore. She soon became his only companion on his scavenging trips, sometimes finding plants among the rocks that his large hands could not grasp.

In addition, Sings Like Rain brought with her a talent for stretching drum skins, something she had learned from her father. She made Wolf Stealer several of his ritual drums and he found that the sound they produced was superior to those he had made himself. This pleased Wolf Stealer for he knew the Spirit of the Drum was evident in the tonal quality and cadence the drum produced. The power of the Drum Spirit is what aids the healer in bringing the lost soul from the Underworld back to the place of the living.

Within a year, Sings Like Rain grew heavy with child and gave birth to a baby girl that Wolf Stealer named Steals my Heart for one look into her deep dark eyes; Wolf Stealer knew that his daughter was the most precious baby he had ever seen. This was saying a lot because it was Wolf Stealer's job to notice the newborn and meditate on the name that Spirit called forth in the child. Wolf Stealer had seen many babies as Shaman, and Steals My Heart was definitely the one he liked the most.

As Steals My Heart grew it became clear that she inherited her father's talent for interpreting dreams. By her tenth birthday she was consulted on many issues of importance in the village in order that she might dream the answer from Spirit. Her father indulged her by teaching her some of the Shaman's ways even though it was not customary to teach these ways to women. She spent a lot of her time helping her father create the herbal tinctures and poultices he used for healing.

About this time, in the wider world, the Indians were beginning to encounter the white man more often, sometimes making trades with them for goods they needed, other times warring with the whites over territory. Wolf Stealer had always been suspicious of the white man. He told the Warrior Chief that he was sure the white man spoke with a forked tongue, telling you one thing while meaning something else entirely.

The Warrior Chief agreed with Wolf Stealer but now that the white man took up more room in the Indian Territory, he felt they were better off making the best of a bad situation and so Wolf Stealer's tribe soon began trading with the white man on a more regular basis. In the Spirit World, Wolf Stealer felt the first inklings that this was not for the best. His dreams were filled with nightmares of demons coming to steal the children of the village. Steals My Heart also had bad dreams, which she relayed to her father in vivid detail. Wolf Stealer, not wishing to scare her, however; explained away the occurrences by teaching her that dreaming nightmares was a natural when the seasons changed. In his heart, however, Wolf Stealer was anything but sure. He wanted to protect the children and so prayed to the Chief of the Sky Spirits for guidance.

In his trance, he was shown how to make a tincture that would help protect the children and the next day set about to gather the herbs and begin the process of making this medicine. That evening, however while he sat by the fire, a woman he knew from the tribe ran to him and throwing herself at his feet bade that he come to help her young son who had fallen ill. Wolf Stealer was often requested at such moments and yet the vehemence with which the woman asked for his help unnerved him slightly. Upon arriving at her wigwam, he greeted the boy's father who sat outside. The woman had been too distraught to explain much of the nature of the illness and so he asked the father many questions to try and get some idea of what was going on in the family.

So often these illnesses stemmed from some issue of the family -- offerings that had not been made, hunting parties that had neglected to leave some of the animal to the Great Spirit in their haste to make it back to camp, or an unresolved hurt between wife and husband. A simple remedy was often had in these cases. The father had little to offer Wolf Stealer of that nature, only saying that the boy had fallen into a deep fever a few hours prior and tossed and turned restlessly.

Wolf Stealer entered the wigwam and had a good look at the boy. He sent everyone else out so he could have some peace and read the boy's spirit. As Wolf Stealer examined him, it was already clear that the boy's soul was in the Underworld. The body was hot and clammy to the touch. The boy's eyes rolled back in his head and no amount of poking would wake him from slumber. Wolf Stealer proceeded to draw back the blanket so he could check the boy over from head to toe, to his horror; however, he discovered the boy was covered with pustules, red and oozing.

Wolf Stealer shouted to the family outside to fetch Sings Like Rain, his herbs, ritual drum and rattles. Healing work

needed to be done and done quickly to save the boy from getting lost forever on the other side. When the flap to the wigwam finally parted it was not Sings Like Rain who entered but his daughter. He was angry with her at first and fearful that she might be taken too. He tried to coax her into going back to her mother. But Steals My Heart stood her ground and insisted on aiding him with the task of covering the pustules with the herbs she had mixed for this purpose.

Wolf Stealer noted to himself that he had maybe been a little too self-indulgent with Steals My Heart and worried that he would have trouble finding a husband for her when the time came. But for now, there was no time to be lost in argument with a self-willed girl. Taking his herbs from his ritual bag, Wolf Stealer tossed them into the fire. Soon the wigwam was filled with an aromatic and heavy smoke. He could feel the effects of the peyote as it entered his lungs and quickly calmed his body. He stood. Steals My Heart took up his rattles, shaking them rhythmically while humming the trance song. Wolf Stealer closed his eyes and began to sing, beating a cadence on his drum; he danced tapping one foot and then the other to the beat.

Wolf Stealer took the path of the Great Eagle to the Underworld. There he searched for the boy. Several times he heard the boy's voice calling to him but as soon as he reached the place where the boy's voice came from, the boy was nowhere to be found. He asked the Spider Queen, who weaved her web and created the great fabric of life, if she had seen the boy. The Spider Queen showed Wolf Stealer a great hole in her web. The faster she spun, the bigger it got. This scared Wolf Stealer a great deal for he knew that something was greatly amiss both in the Spirit World and in his own. His job now was to locate the young boy as quickly as possible not to spend time solving the larger issues and so he continued searching.

By morning, he left the Underworld in order to see to the health of the boy. While he had been unable to find the boy's spirit, he knew that the worst cases sometimes required several trips to complete the healing. To his dismay, however, it became clear that the boy had worsened in the night and by midday, the boy passed into the long night, forever lost in the Underworld. The tribe mourned. The women of his family wailed. The great Warrior Chief consoled the village.

Wolf Stealer wasted no time in continuing work on his healing tincture and yet these things could not be rushed. The herbs needed to boil for several days in order that the healing powers would leech into the water properly and the magic could be performed. Wolf Stealer prayed to the Chief of the Sky Spirits asking for his forgiveness. He made an offering to the Great Spirit in the name of his tribe knowing that something was out of alignment between the Spirit World and the earthly one.

By the following evening, two more children were ill and one of the elders of the tribe succumbed. Family members of the sick and dying joined Wolf Stealer in the sweat lodge so that they could purge the evil spirits from the tribe and heal the sick. Several hours into the ceremony and a loud knock came to the door. Wolf Stealer could hear voices calling to him and ignored them at first because they disturbed the sanctity of the sweat. Voices continued to be raised outside the lodge and Wolf Stealer could no longer ignore the commotion. He raised himself and opened the door.

Sings Like Rain ran to him and he noticed other members of his family standing in the clearing near the lodge as well. His wife motioned for him to come quickly and now he knew something was really wrong because she of all people knew the sacredness of the lodge. He left the others to continue the ceremony and ran to his wigwam.

Inside, Steals My Heart was wrapped in her bed blanket, tossing and turning from fever. Upon looking her over, he found the same red pustules he had seen on the boy a few days before. His heart sank. How he wished he could turn back time and make his daughter return to the safety of his home. It was his fault -- he should have been stronger with her, he was too indulgent, he spoiled her too much and now look at her!

Sheba came to sit near Steals My Heart and nudged her gently, licking at her face. Sheba too felt the disturbance in the village, and slumped, head on paws, next to Steals My Heart. Anyone other than Wolf Stealer who ventured too close to the girl heard Sheba's low growl of protective warning.

Wolf Stealer sat and stared at the boiling tincture. Maybe if he just rushed it this once, everything would be all right. He prayed to the Great Spirit and asked Spirit to help him to save his daughter, who was his life, the one who stole his heart. Carefully, he lifted the boiling pot and strained the frothy liquid into a bowl to cool. He knew that the herbs should really boil until morning but what if his daughter did not make it? What if others became ill? He had to do something to save his tribe and all eyes were on him, were they not?

Once the tincture cooled, he bade the women bring a cup for their families and he divided the tincture amongst them, saving enough for his daughter. Steals My Heart was deep in the Underworld but he opened her mouth and made her swallow. When she had finished, Wolf Stealer put his rattles around his ankles and carrying his drum went out to the village fire. The Warrior Chief was sitting in counsel there and greeted Wolf Stealer as he entered the Sacred Circle. The Warrior Chief told Wolf Stealer that he was grateful for his healing powers and knew that if anyone could find a way through this, it was Wolf Stealer, the man who had stolen a wolf cub from its own mother so long ago.

Wolf Stealer thanked the Chief but his heart was heavy. His own daughter was ill. Had he angered the Great Spirit by telling her about the ways of Shaman? As Wolf Stealer entered trance, he began to hear the voices of the demons, the ones from his dreams and they frightened him. Maybe he was not as good a shaman priest as everyone thought? Who was he to think that he could heal anyone? He began to drum and felt the call of the Underworld, pulling him further and further into trance.

The sound of the men talking and the crackle of the fire ebbed and flowed around him. His voice hummed and sang lifting his vibration level higher and higher. In this place, Wolf Stealer said to the Great Spirit, "If you make her live, I will do your bidding. I will not teach her the Shaman ways for she is a woman. I have angered you." Long after the fire had died down, Wolf Stealer was in trance, determined to save the village and his precious Heart.

But by morning, the children had grown worse. Two more of the village elders entered the long rest. The village was in mourning and the people were wondering what they had done to so anger the Great Spirit. Wolf Stealer had no answers. He could only hang his head and wonder himself. Nothing he did appeared to be working. The tingles of chaos were hammering in his brain. In trance, he had seen the Great Web empty; the Spider Queen had deserted her people and left her web in tatters. Wolf Stealer was despondent. None of his training had prepared him for what he was experiencing and he pushed aside the questions, choosing to remain in seclusion.

Holding his daughter's hand, he sang to her and tried to call her soul from the Underworld. Her hands were cold now, the life force disappearing from her body. He urged her to come back to him, he begged her. He asked for her forgiveness for being such a bad father. He should have known better. He should have never let her train in the priest's ways and instead prepared her to be a good wife and mother. Sings Like Rain wailed outside with the other women. The village had come to a standstill. No one ate, no one harvested the corn, which sat rotting on the stalk and no one went hunting.

By morning, Wolf Stealer still clung to his daughter's hand. Her body was cold and stiff now. The life force had gone to the Spirit World never to return. His wife begged him to come out and eat what little food she could prepare for him. He had work to do. There was hope in the village. One of the children appeared improved; the child's sores had begun to dry up and go hard. Sings Like Rain needed to clean the body of her daughter and prepare her for burial. Wolf Stealer shoved her away, tears in his eyes and told her to leave him be.

The Warrior Chief came into the wigwam. He observed the scene and knew Wolf Stealer might be lost to the village if he continued in this way. The Chief counseled Wolf Stealer to resume his healing ceremonies. The men waited in the lodge for Wolf Stealer's direction. There was still time and their luck could turn. Again, Wolf Stealer shook his head. He pointed to his lifeless daughter and with tears streaming down his face said, "She stole my heart and took it with her to the Spirit World, just as she stole it when she arrived here. I cannot leave her. I will dress her myself. I am useless. Find another priest to help you. The Great Spirit is angry with me."

The Warrior Chief shook his head and left the wigwam hoping Wolf Stealer would see reason soon. As a result of Wolf Stealer's absence, Sings Like Rain took over the healing. She began work on another batch of tincture. Years living with Wolf Stealer had taught her much about the herbs he used for healing. Still with grieving in her heart, she placed her energy into healing the sick and returning the tribe to normal, hoping that her endeavors would save as many as possible.

Night and day she worked, bathing the sick and singing for their return from the Underworld. Cleaning sores, administering herbs, creating tincture. The work was tiring and seemingly endless. With many of the tribe's hunters sick or dead, food was scarce. The available women and men who were not sick were foraging for food, tending to relatives and burying the dead in the sacred mounds. Friends and family left this world sometimes quicker than Sings Like Rain could get to them. She grieved them all. A large hole grew in her heart and yet she continued. What else could she do?

Wolf Stealer stayed by his wigwam lost in despair, his daughter buried and his heart, broken. The fire had long gone out but the cold of the fall air did nothing to rouse him from his stupor. He berated himself for all the things he had done wrong and swore he could hear the demons and the Chief of the Sky Spirits do the same. Wolf Stealer heard not the crying of the children who were falling sick each day. He cared not that his wife was working herself to the bone. Several times the Warrior Chief tried in vain to wake him from this stupor and call him back to the land of the living but Wolf Stealer wanted to hear none of the man's platitudes.

A great anger brewed in his heart now. The beating of the second heart, the heart of the tribe grew faint and Wolf Stealer wished only that it would disappear from his senses forever.

"How dare you!" he screamed at the Great Spirit. "How dare you take her after all I have done for you? You promised to keep her well if I changed my ways. Now you have cursed me. I want nothing more to do with any of you!"

Tired and hungry, Sings Like Rain, could hold off the tide of the illness no longer; it flooded through the village like a wild fire. She fell ill one night and by morning she was cold and gone. The Warrior Chief knew that even his wisdom might not be enough to save the tribe. The families of the village grew smaller by the day. Wolf Stealer, upon hearing of the death of his wife, only grew more withdrawn. The night she died, he stole away to the white man's village and traded the last of his drum skins for some of that whiskey they loved so much. The heat of the liquid burned his throat but before long the numbing quality lifted the ache of his heart just enough to help him sleep through the night.

By the following week, the entire village had the illness, even the wise Warrior Chief lay on his pallet covered in sores. No one tended the village fire circle. No one conducted ceremonies in the empty sweat lodge. No one cooked food or made healing herbs. And by now, drunk with whiskey, the shaman priest, no longer heard the beat of the tribe's heart next to his own. Lifting one droopy eyelid and raising his bottle to the sky, the priest gave silent thanks to the Chief of the Sky Spirits for relieving him of such a burden. One by one, the sick died, left to rot in their own beds. No one was well enough or cared enough to bury them in the sacred mounds.

White men from the neighboring town smelled the stench on the wind one day and came looking to see what was going on in the Ojibwa village. What they found were flies and death. The whole village decimated. When they approached one of the wigwams, they heard the growl of a wolf, long and steady emanating from inside. One of the men parted the doorway only to find himself smothered with the menacing form of a large she-wolf, her teeth bared and ready to kill. Luckily, the man's brother had his wits about him and raising his musket, shot the wolf dead.

Everyone in the posse was relieved; the wolf was probably scavenging for food, they conjectured. Once inside, they found one drunk Indian still alive and sleeping it off. They all looked at each other and laughed, releasing the tension from moments before. Probably avoided the illness from being so cooked with whiskey, they thought.

The leader of the group poked at the drunken Indian with his gun and told him to get up. The Indian opened his

eyes but did not move. The man took this as a sign of insolence and slapped him across the face with the butt of his gun. Wolf Stealer, his name lost along with his tribe, would not answer any of the man's questions. The men shrugged at this behavior and decided to call the drunk, Ol' Whiskey Red for convenience. They used their torches and burned what was left of the village, no point in letting this case of smallpox travel to the town.

Ol' Red as he soon came to be called in town spent his days begging for alms so he could buy himself more whiskey. The villagers made fun of him, and sometimes passersby would spit in his face or throw their slop jars on his head. He stank. By the time winter came and the heavy snows blanketed the village, Ol' Red took to hiding under stairs and in barns to keep warm. One night, however, he was caught and thrown out of his hiding place. None of the townsfolk wanted a stinky Indian living in their barn. Who knew what kind of disease a guy like that could bring? There were also rumors that he had the devil in him, after all how had he survived the smallpox when everyone else in his tribe had died?

The following morning, the innkeeper found Ol' Red underneath the stairwell, half covered in snow, holding his bottle of whiskey in one hand, and something else... a dirty and worn rattle, in the other. Ol' Red had frozen to death in the night but how curious to be holding that rattle, the innkeeper thought. They buried Ol' Red in an unmarked grave south of town with his rattle and his bottle of whiskey. And soon after, no one gave Ol' Red another thought and his story and that of his tribe became lost to history...

III

A great silence fell over the room where Joanie and her grandfather were sitting. She waited for him to continue but he did not. "Are you telling me that this story has to do with those two fairies? I just don't get it? It's a terrible story, everyone dies!"

Joanie's grandfather looked over at her before speaking. "I told you it was a long story and you are right, everyone died. Life was hard back then and Wolf Stealer made a grave mistake that he paid for do you know what it was?"

Joanie shook her head.

Grandfather continued, "Wolf Stealer was overcome with the loss of his daughter and thought the Great Spirit was angry with him for teaching her the ways of the Shaman. His anger and animosity grew when Spirit appeared to refuse his prayers by taking his only daughter, Steals My Heart, which blinded him to the needs in the village.

But the problem was not that he taught his daughter about healing, for any inspiration of the heart is the voice of God but that when asked repeatedly to put aside his feelings and care for the heart of the tribe, he refused to do so. He became consumed with hatred and self-loathing and as a result could not hear the voice of the Spirit World over his own self-doubt. The spirit of his daughter was with him whispering in his ear but he pushed her voice aside thinking that Great Spirit was only playing with his feelings.

If he had listened he would have heard her urging him to place his love for her and his grief over her death into the healing of the children and the tribe members that were left behind. You see Joanie, only love is real and the power of love is stronger than disease and illness. He had a powerful love for his daughter, which when directed to the healing work of the tribe may have healed his own heart as well."

"You mean he could have saved the tribe?" Joanie asked.

"I believe it was possible, Joanie and more importantly it would have been the pathway of his highest calling. If he saw beyond his own grief and anger he would have noticed that his tinctures and his healing work had already begun to heal the spirit of the tribe. He may have heard the words of his daughter in his ear rather than those pesky demons, which were getting him off track and poured the love that overwhelmed his heart into the healing of the children who needed him so badly. I think doing so would have given him what he needed to heal the loss and pain

within him, too.

Nevertheless, Wolf Stealer and the members of his tribe were a part of a bigger trend in western civilization, Joanie -- the colonization by the western mindset, which was changing tribal culture in unexpected and devastating ways. Perhaps the larger movement of forces was more powerful at the time than Wolf Stealer's heart and really beyond his immediate control. In the end, some lessons are only learned over many lifetimes for everyone involved in the complex relationship between all beings."

"But what does this story have to do with those two fairies? Other than I see the wolf mask, rattle and drum must be Wolf Stealer's?"

"Good question and I will answer it as I continue the story. For I told you it was a long one and there is more yet to come."

"More, but everyone is dead. How can there be more?"

"Patience is a virtue Joanie."

Joanie rolled her eyes but sat back on the pillow to wait for her grandfather to continue the story.

"As you know, Joanie from our talks, what dies must live again. And this was no different for the spirit of Wolf Stealer..."

IV

Over a century and many turnings of the wheel of time came between the death of Ol' Red in that village in Wisconsin and the time his spirit was born again in the body of another in a city far, far away from the site of that Ojibwa village. This is how the Spirit World and the earthly world work in harmony for lessons must be learned and Wolf Stealer died having walked away from love, consumed with self-loathing, fear and hatred.

Wolf Stealer had yet another name now. He was born into a Jewish family far removed from the life he led as a Native American shaman priest. His father was known in the world of entertainment and his mother was a housewife. And yet, once a soul has an experience, that experience is remembered on some part of that soul's being for eternity. It is one aspect of karma - the stories we carry with us through time.

That is not to say that we remember these things outright, more often than not we have no idea who we once were in other lifetimes. Some people even believe they only live once and this once is the only chance they get to live an earthly existence. Others know differently, sensing something bigger than just one lifetime, even if they do not remember the details of their past existences.

The young boy grew and by the time he was in school, the call of his soul beckoned to him. But you have to remember, he recalled nothing of his time in that Ojibwa village and he was not taught the ways of the Shaman in his current life.

The call in his soul took on a different form, one that is accepted and known in the modern world. One day he was watching a music show on TV, the guy in the back of the jazz band playing the drums caught his eye and he felt the flutter in his heart of the distant memory. The man's drumsticks tapping the rhythm fascinated the boy and the cadence lulled him into reverie. That very day he asked his mother if she would get him drum lessons for his birthday. His mother wanted very much to please him. His father had left home when he was four after an affair and she saw the pain of this abandonment in the boy's eyes. Maybe just maybe he would have something to keep his mind off things and keep out of trouble. She agreed to the lessons.

The boy was a natural, of course. He held the beat in his heart. Some part of him knew it was a gift and as he grew in talent, he grew to see himself as an artist with something important to offer the world. But a soul does not just remember the good times and the talents; the soul remembers the way it coped once as well. This is so that the soul can be given the opportunity to overcome the limitations it once placed on itself and learn the lessons it failed to learn in the previous lifetime.

This boy's ego grew with his talent mimicking the self-absorption of Wolf Stealer's last days. He enjoyed the attention he received just as much as he enjoyed playing. He was courted by the best teachers and given opportunities others failed to achieve. He saw himself as unique and somewhat beyond reproach. To others he appeared to have it all together. His friends envied the fact that a great jazz master taught him and they wondered amongst themselves at that magical quality that the boy's playing sometimes evoked. What was it he had and they did not? He did not seem to be just playing but channeling something greater than himself. He was, as we know, a great healer and shaman, even if he did not remember it consciously.

Inside, however, this boy was lonely and afraid. What if God took away this talent? What if people realized he was not talented at all but a fraud and all of this attention went away? It could right? On visits with his father, he saw a man who appeared to be successful. He had a good job in entertainment. He had women. He had the respect of his colleagues and the community.

But at the same time, the boy did not respect this man who had left him and his mother over an affair with another woman. There was unresolved pain in the boy's heart because of this abandonment by his father. The pain reawakened his feelings of overwhelming loss from another time and of feeling like he could not control the outcome of life no matter how hard he tried.

The boy carried a story that said -- love is fickle and people who say they love each other only end up hurting the ones they love. He believed this wholeheartedly underneath it all and embraced the tenant in his life. As a result, he resolved that he would control his feelings. He would not let strong emotions get in the way of what he wanted and so he closed off his heart and chose to live in a form of darkness where feelings come second to desire and want.

As the boy grew into a teenager, his father sensing the divide between them thought that he could remedy it by allowing his son a taste of life in the big city. Maybe if he acted more like a friend than a father, his son would show him love and respect. The young man's father failed to realize that his son cared not about love nor did he respect the decisions his father had made. The father desperate to get a positive response gave the boy his first joint, thinking that he might ingratiate himself into his son's good graces and initiate him into adulthood. While the boy smoked the joint, his soul remembered on some level a moment a long time ago when smoking Peyote was something sacred and revered. He thought he understood this feeling, after all, all great musicians, including his teacher smoked the weed so surely he would too.

Smoking marijuana was what musicians did. The high was what gave them creative juices, brought them down from a show and allowed them to play the music -- right? He forgot in his haste to judge his own perception that there was only one true source of creativity and joy – Spirit. And he never bothered to learn what might be other more creative and fulfilling ways to relax after a long concert.

The young man saw that his friends noticed him and idolized him, they wanted to be a part of his world more than anything, so he stole a stash of his father's weed and they all smoked a bowl and from then on his reputation as a real musician grew. He also saw that his mother was relieved that by buying him a new drum set and lessons with a famous jazz drummer, he seemed less focused on the fact that his father was remarrying and moving to the east coast. Feeling this way allowed her to ignore the signs that something was not quite right.

The boy learned to hone this persona, he played the part and everyone in his life believed him to be the talented musician who knew where he was going and how he was going to get there. The more he played the part the more he was confident people bought it and soon he bought the act himself. He was confident. He was talented. The chicks loved him and by the time he turned a man, he had started seeing that being in a woman's bed was an

important part of being a musician as well.

The women loved the fact that he looked at them while he played and played with them in the dark. They adored him and told him how great he was, how talented he seemed to be and how they knew he was going to make it. He was wasn't he? There was no way but up. He gave the women just enough attention to make them think love was involved but not enough to get tied down. When anyone argued with him that there was something missing in his life, maybe it was a woman who wanted more than casual sex or his mother suggesting he might want to think of security, he laughed.

After all, he was a stoner, a musician, a drummer and he had talent, man! "Fuck 'em! Fuck 'em all," he would say as he found another woman to sleep with at the bar where he had played that night, another someone who he would call his new girlfriend, for awhile, anyway.

"Who needs 'em," he thought while not answering his mother's repeated phone calls to check on the status of that job interview he had forgotten to go to. "They just don't get me."

In high school, he had smoked pot daily and loved the feeling of being high. He saw the world in bright colors and it appealed to him when he sucked from that bowl or ate the ganja food. He could write music that meant something to him in that place...when the time was right. If he was not high he was bored. Bored with the life his parent's led, bored with the rules, bored with school...just plain bored.

The mother let the young man drop out of school after repeated trips to the principal's office for bad behavior and even worse grades. The people at school did not get him either. All these rules. All these expectations. Who needed that shit? His mother wanted so badly for her son to be happy, to love her as he used to do as a small child -- unconditionally and without the moody reservation. She wanted his insolence to stop. Maybe if he did not go to school and got his GED and did his own thing for awhile, he would get over this phase and get on with his life. Find a career he liked, settle down. She could only hope.

The musician had his mind set -- after all, musicians and artists live by a different code, right? What other people think does not matter and what is more, good art is about freedom, not about being in some lame box that people with broken dreams create. He would very often tell his mother that he was a musician and musicians make money by playing music not by putting on a suit. She would sigh to herself on the way to work each morning and keep praying that he would come around soon.

To those who did not look too hard or ask too many questions, this young man was headed for great things. These people enjoyed being around him because they thought they could ride his coattails to the top, bask in the glow of someone who looked successful and did what he wanted when they could not. Or they just plain did not give a damn.

Riding on this wave, the young man chose to go to New York for college. No one could stop him now! He would be among the best of the best. He saw himself famous. He saw himself surrounded by women, not just any women though. He wanted women of quality. Girls he could talk to about philosophy and poetry. Artists and filmmakers. Yeah, maybe he would make a few films too.

In New York people are honest, brutally honest. Before long, the man found himself being asked the tough questions. Who are you? What do you want? He no longer had that network around him of high school friends who imagined their lives lived vicariously through him. People wanted real, gritty and deep, not a façade that they could poke a hole through. He got some attention but not the same attention. In music school the requirements were tough and exacting. The day he showed up to class stoned, the teacher noticed almost immediately and told him to come back when he was ready to be serious.

But he was serious wasn't he? He was going to make it and no one could tell him otherwise. He was pissed-off that these has-been teachers had the audacity to make him defend creative expression and personal choices. His

talent was obvious and he probably could teach these classes in his sleep. As a result of these early experiences at college, the man soon became more withdrawn from people at school and spent time with the cats at the clubs who didn't trip on him about form and function. He smoked pot with these dudes and talked music. He did not play there often but he talked about playing there with the likes of Wynton Marsalis and Dave Brubeck.

The guys who hung around at these clubs got excited because not too many people were good enough to make it in the business. This man appeared to have that something special, that indefinable quality which would convince anyone that he was going to make it -- one day. This man's world was about to crash in on him, however. The years of pot smoking and spiritual disharmony of the soul had left his brain chemistry unable to function like normal and he was smoking pot more often now that school was not going so well. The fast lifestyle he led -- drinking at the bars at night, not sleeping or eating properly, smoking pot and cigarettes were really signs of his ailing spirit.

A spirit that craved more and somewhere deep inside knew better. He fell into an illness of the mind and when he never showed up for class or work, he lost his place in school and lost his job. The doctors called it Manic Depression or Bi-Polar and whatever other fancy names they could give his parents. They described his problem as a mental illness that causes the sufferer to cycle between episodes of mania and depression or in other words, from being really hyped up like being on lots of coffee being really low and unhappy.

The common treatment is to give people a drug called Lithium. While Lithium is naturally present in the body, unnaturally administered by pills, it can have many negative effects. After taking the pills for a few weeks, the man ended up suffering from many of these negative effects and so refused to take them any longer.

He convinced himself that if he just cleaned up his lifestyle for a while, moved back home from New York to California and got his shit together, he would be fine. And that is exactly what he proceeded to do...

V

Joanie looked at her grandfather quizzically, "And then he was OK?"

"Let me ask you. In the entire story I have told about this man up until now, have you seen the signs that he learned any lessons about his situation?"

"Not really. He just seems to be doing the same thing he always did. He thinks he knows better than everyone including God, I think."

"You are right. He just runs away from his problems, which if you remember back to the story of Wolf Stealer, is the lesson he neglected to learn in that lifetime. He was too afraid to face what was hard so he ignored it." Grandfather continued the story.

VI

At home, the young man went back to life as normal. Again, he had the appearance of having gotten his life together as by now he was pretty adept and having the appearance of being exactly what everyone wanted for him. They saw and felt his talent and his drive and assumed they understood him. He desired to please them and when those around him were excited about his career, he felt he could do everything he said he was going to do.

So he chose a college degree that his mother thought would get him a good job after school and his father thought would be better than nothing and he continued his life. And yet, there was more to this man than just a façade. Remember he is Wolf Stealer, and Wolf Stealer was a very talented healer and Shaman. These qualities were in the young man as well but underdeveloped in this lifetime.

Sometimes he found himself walking in nature and really feeling connected to the life force we call God. He gravitated toward spiritual readings, gardening and other Eastern or Native philosophies. Something in him yearned for more. That which is God within us will always try to bring us back to God and it was no different for this young man. If we are ready to heed the call, the lessons will flow naturally. If we have ignored the lessons, the move toward our highest potential will come at great personal cost and upheaval. And sometimes, despite our best efforts, we have a long way to go to reach our highest potential.

The day arrived when destiny and healing showed up on the same path as the young man walked. Unbeknownst to him, another person he loved walked the path of life at this moment. This woman was already a healer in this lifetime and had learned the lessons related to what happens when you ignore your true calling and the truth that lies within. She also had something to say, even though she was not yet aware, to a man she had loved through the bounds of time and space.

When they met at a party, sparks flew and they recognized each other immediately as soulmates often do. A great connection happened and it happened quickly. Neither the man nor the woman new of the lifetime in the Ojibwa village yet, they just felt a strong energetic connection and found themselves gravitating toward each other. Wolf Stealer's daughter, reborn now in another body, thought she understood the nature of this connection, obviously some sort of past life relationship and at first, thought the man understood this connection just as well.

The man on the other hand, mistook the connection as just another time when someone, a woman, recognized his talent and admired him. He assumed he could handle this meeting like he had handled countless others but he was wrong. The woman, ready for love, gave this man her heart. For she knew he was special to her and that she had traveled a long way to be with him again. Deep inside her soul was a voice, a voice that wanted very much to tell him all the things he needed to know in person, all the things he had not heard when she was a spirit so long ago. The spirit he had ignored.

Maybe just maybe she could reach him this time. But she was afraid of losing him again as well and the man did nothing to assuage that fear because for him nothing in his life was serious apart from where he thought he was going. The man underestimated one thing about this new connection, however; you see the woman believed in the Goddess. She was a powerful witch and shaman. She had developed these skills for many years now and recognized this encounter as a challenge from God.

She prayed and meditated on her fear and the Goddess said:

"Love him with all your heart. Do not hold back. For only love is real."

So she did just that. She spilled her heart and allowed love to flow between them without reservation. The man understood energy, even if he did not know how to use it effectively, after all energy working had once been an important part of his life as a shaman priest. He had closed himself off from love a long time ago, some would say before the lifetime he led now, afraid that love hurt and those you love only abandoned you or disappeared.

This feeling had only been heightened by his childhood experience and when he felt the love from this woman come so naturally and effortlessly he became mired in fear and anger. He had no idea how to handle all the feelings she brought up for him. He pushed her away in as cruel a fashion as he could think of without damaging the image of himself as the nice guy musician who has it all together. He told her that she was not a part of his vision for the future. She was mistaken. He insisted nothing they had experienced together was intended to be serious.

But in reality, it was too late to escape the spiritual journey he was about to embark upon -- he had been touched deeply within his soul and a new story of healing was about to emerge. The man recognized this woman - she felt familiar -- and he had trouble pushing down the feeling that she was not the same as all the other women he had met and slept with. He had already started smoking pot again and now he went back to it like a crutch in an effort to drown the feelings of overwhelming love he had felt by the dull roar of a cool high. He was safe in that place and found himself able to ignore the confusing feelings surrounding this new woman.

The woman persevered. She could not let go of the idea that this meeting was more than a simple mistake. She prayed and meditated. And that is when she first met the Warrior King or Chief. He came to her in a vision. He showed her the tribe where she had come from and he told her the story of Wolf Stealer.

In the vision, this Spirit Guide brought the young man to the sweat lodge on the spirit plane and showed him how he had misused the sacred peyote with his callous disregard for what pot did to his body and his mind and his Spirit. The Warrior Chief asked the woman to be the man's healer and with love in her heart she agreed. He had already entered a manic cycle of his disease process and his erratic behavior began to make his friends and family take notice and this time, he had a spiritual guide to help him on the path to healing.

The story of their healing journey is one I will leave for another time. Let us just say that to heal is to be healed. Before they parted ways again for a while, the two of them were changed forever. You see the healing power of love and the inspirational power of music are very strong forces that move great blocks of fear and doubt and allow the strength of Spirit to flow naturally once again.

The young man was to re-confront the demons inside, those demons that haunted him from the time of Wolf Stealer. It was the woman healer who recognized that what modern medicine called manic depression was a split in the soul between the desires of the ego or lower self and the needs of the soul or higher self to express its highest potential. Build strong enough walls between those two aspects of self and sooner or later a great split occurs. Her goal was to help him bring those two parts of himself together so he could live from a place of highest potential and release the need to fight within.

With all his pot smoking, he had not matured spiritually or personally. Everything he did was on the surface and for a long time he had liked it that way. But this situation is similar to placing a lid on a boiling pot of water, at some point the power of the steam will blow the lid off. The power of his own spirit blew the lid off the façade and it was time for him to learn all the things about life and love that he had avoided for so long, the hard way like everyone else.

What she did not realize at first was that he changed her too. He brought music into her life and he opened up the center in her that was love. Helping him through his illness enabled her to see that she was good enough to be a healer and good enough to deserve healing herself. She became inspired to write poetry and stories and she would later write a book about their experiences together. The natural flow of spirit was restored in her as well and she became one with her own powerful talent as an artist. The musician pushed her to seek adventure and take care of the teenager she had once been and that still lived inside her and who had never had the opportunity to grow into a woman…

VII

Grandfather finished his story and took one look at his watch. "Girl, we're going to be late if we sit here telling stories too much longer. You run to the big house and get dressed and I'll meet you up there."

"Late for what Grandfather?" Joanie looked at her grandfather like he had two heads. She was still trying to figure out who was who and how this story applied to the old man in front of her.

"The memorial service is what. You are going with me."

With that, Joanie was pushed out the door of her grandfather's studio in the direction of the big house. Joanie was definitely going to have to write her own mystery novel when this was all over.

Joanie's Mom helped her find her blue suit, the one she wore when they went to tea at Mrs. Jacobs a few weeks ago. She dressed quickly, checking her hair and make-up in the mirror. At thirteen, Joanie's biggest complaint

was that her parents still treated her like a kid and that is why she liked to spend time with Grandfather, he of all people was straight with her and treated her like he knew she could handle things. Today, however, there were lots of emotions swimming around in her heart and in her soul. Her body was abuzz with a sadness she could not entirely explain away. The story her grandfather told her replayed in her head and she realized her issues with Whiptail this week, paled in comparison to the human tragedy of love and loss and redemption in those stories. No wonder he needed his space!

Her ramblings on the day of "The Call" must have seemed shallow and self-absorbed. Joanie started to wonder what her contribution to the world was going to be. Her grandfather had often tried to teach her some of the shaman's ways. He would ask her to pay attention to the flight of the butterfly or tell him about her dreams. He learned these ways, she knew now from this woman called The Empress. He had his altar, his incense, his medicine drum. Her father thought it was all a little peculiar so they had chosen to live away from Grandfather until her mother finally decided Grandfather was too old to live alone. As a result, they had seen him only on vacations and holidays up until now.

Listening to those stories today made Joanie realize that maybe her Grandfather knew some things about life that her parents did not. After all, if Wolf Stealer's next life proved anything, it was how easily you could become removed from the truth and avoid your calling and the love you had to give to others. If she learned something today it was that she was not going to make the same mistake that young man made, whoever he was. She was going to learn the ways of the shaman and heal others, in whatever form that took for her.

Joanie met her grandfather at the limo and they sat in silence most of the way to the hall where the memorial service was being held. She had all these questions about the stories he had told of Wolf Stealer and the young man. Whatever happened to that man? Did he get well or go back to smoking pot? What happened to the healer? She knew now that those two people were depicted in the drawing he had received that morning.

The drum player and the healer woman as fairies with love coming out of her wand and music coming out of his. There was still so much mystery and so many questions she longed to ask. Nevertheless she kept these questions to herself for the time being, she would have plenty of time to ask Grandfather later.

Joanie was surprised to see the number of people that were sitting in the large hall ready to say their goodbyes. The security men at the door checked IDs and reporters flashed pictures and asked a barrage of incessant questions to invitees entering the hall. Who was this woman, exactly? Joanie had been piecing the information together for some time but instead of having the answers she sought, Joanie only had more questions. The drawing, the stories, the past lives, the scrapbooks. It was as if history was twisting in on itself, the chain of energy that held life expanding and becoming more complicated. Truth, Joanie thought, sure came with a lot of responsibility. The Empress had been Grandpa's business partner, a well-known, well-respected leader. An artist and friend. Her life was complete, and yet it was not really over. The woman's influence extended into this room, filling people's hearts and minds. Joanie realized that her life was affected even though she could not remember meeting the woman.

She saw people in the seats she recognized from her grandfather's studio and from television or movies she had seen. Wow! This was cool. It was like being at some fancy award show. Some of these people waved at her grandfather as the ushers took them to their seats.

As the memorial program began, Joanie listened as person after person recalled events from this woman's life. She had been a writer, a filmmaker, and a great healer. She seemed to have touched many people's lives. A few of the speakers laughed and joked and others told poignant stories of how she helped them through difficulty.

Grandfather's tears spilled down his cheeks when he heard these stories. Joanie handed him a tissue box that someone passed to her and he blew his nose very loudly on several occasions. The woman's grown children talked about their childhood and about love. Her daughter said, "Only love is real." Joanie recognized that caption from the story her grandfather had told her earlier.

When the ceremony and speeches were over, the invitees were asked to join the family in a large tent outside for refreshments. People were standing around meeting each other and laughing, telling old stories about this time or that time that they had spent with the woman who had died.

While her grandfather and Joanie were in line for food, a man approached them that she recognized as one of the speakers, the woman's son, Galen. Galen was around fifty, looked somewhat like his Mom from her younger days. He had a warm face and wore a black suit with a purple sash. Strangely enough his brown eyes had that same piercing quality that her grandfather's did, as though he could reach in and...know your thoughts, Joanie concluded.

"Benjamin?"

Her grandfather smiled at the man, "Galen, how's your family?"

"Great sir, we're waiting for you to come and visit. Anytime you like. I know my wife would love to see you again and the kids – Pete's finishing college, Meredith's a high school senior – I know they'd like to see you. You are one of Mom's oldest friends and I think of you like family and so speaking for all of us, I'd like you to know that our door is always open." At that point he noticed Joanie. "And this must be your granddaughter, Joanie?"

"Yes, since my wife died. You remember Rachel, my daughter; she came to live with me at the house with her family."

"Joanie you didn't get to meet my mother did you?"

"Not exactly. I have seen pictures though."

"Well then, if your grandfather doesn't mind, I will take you over to the table in the back there with the memorabilia. You can see the photos of your grandfather and my mother working at the production company."

Joanie followed Galen to the back of the tent where the family had set-up a memorial table. She instantly recognized Grandfather from the time he was a young man working at this big computer and one where he was playing drums in a hall somewhere. That photo reminded her quite a bit of that guy in the drawing. Interesting, she thought.

"That's your grandfather working at the non-linear editor back in the early days of the company he founded with Mom, Joanie," Galen said pointing to the picture of her grandfather at the computer. "You know, of course they made films there and your grandfather was in charge of the music and sound editing."

Joanie looked around the table at all the photos and memorabilia. There were even a couple Oscars displayed in cases for some films that Joanie recognized the names of since her grandfather had shown these to her a few times in his home theater. Galen pointed out this older lady who was shaking hands with a past U.S. president and other famous people as his mother.

"Come down here, Joanie, you can see a picture of Mom as a young woman before she started the production company." Galen pointed at a photo in an ornate frame.

Joanie took a good look at the picture Galen was pointing to and did a double take. She could not believe her eyes. Now everything was clear. The fairy in the drawing was Galen's Mom! The woman smiling back from the picture looked exactly like the woman in the drawing – long brown hair, beautiful pink lips and she was even wearing a silly fairy costume like it was Halloween, or something. Putting two and two together with the stories she had heard in the service, a flood of realization hit Joanie like a ton of brick. She must be the healer. The one in the story who helped the young man.

"Galen. People said your Mom did healing, what did that mean?"

"Well, yes, Joanie, Mom was a life coach and healer, especially early in her career before the production company took a lot of her time. She worked with people doing something called soul retrieval, which is based on old Shamanic teachings. But you know, Joanie, your grandfather and she later founded as part of their company, a charitable organization that provided healing work for those in need."

Galen picked up one of the many books authored by his Mom on the table. "This one they wrote together about the work they did all over the world. Your grandfather was one of my Mom's students, actually. They came together again when he was healing and realized he needed spiritual guidance. They ended up doing a lot of work with people suffering from mental illness using the techniques she originally used with him. Today, people treat mental illness very differently in no small part because of the work they did together to raise awareness on a new perspective of this disease."

Joanie had seen the book before but never paid much attention. Now she could not believe that her own grandfather had really done all these interesting things. He never really said anything about his work, not like this. She wondered now if he had held back, not wanting to impose his own beliefs on her. Now the medicine drum made much more sense. Of course, he would be honored by native healers for his work.

Galen flipped through to the part of the book with the photos of her grandfather and his Mom doing work in Africa and other countries. They were young and smiling. This must have been the time period depicted in her grandmother's scrapbooks. The family story was making a lot more sense now, sort of.

"You know, they spent so much time together why didn't they just marry each other?" Joanie asked suddenly.

Galen looked down at Joanie and chuckled. "That's a good question Joanie. You know, you are a bright young woman so I think I can say this to you. There are some people in the world who love each other very much and do very powerful things together but for some reason they are just not meant to be together that way." After a pause Galen added with a shrug, "In this lifetime anyway."

At that point, Galen looked up from the table and Joanie turned to see that her grandfather was making his way over.

"Benjamin you have an amazing granddaughter. We've had a really good conversation here, so when you come to visit you can bring her too. I am sure she would like to come ride the horses."

Joanie's eyes got really big at the mention of her favorite subject. "Is that possible, Grandfather?"

Joanie's grandfather laughed, heartily. "I suppose so, Joanie, we'll go to Galen's ranch together but we'll have to ask your Mom's permission first, okay?"

"Well, Joanie, it was great meeting you and I am sure we will see each other soon," Galen said, "I have to go talk to some other people but you keep asking those great questions, we'll make a coach of you before long."

Joanie smiled. She thought she knew what he meant too. Maybe asking good questions is part of being a healer like her grandfather and his friend. At that point, Joanie turned and continued to look at the table a little longer. Her grandfather came up to her side. The look on his face was a familiar one in recent days; he was lost in the annuals of memory and time. Something caught her eye. Another book. The title flashed in her mind like a stroke of lightening, opening up a vast chasm of understanding. She looked back at her grandfather just as he put his hand on her shoulder. He smiled that knowing smile and gave her a wink. Something passed between them that she would carry with her the rest of her life.

"Joanie, I put the food on that table over there," he said pointing across the room, "I am hungry, let's go eat."

Woodland Jazz Club
Benjamin and Mullberry
PLAYING TONIGHT
Anywhere But Here...

Joanie took one final look at the pictures on the memorial table and then up at her grandfather. "Grandfather?" "Yes, Joanie."

"I think you are a really magical person."

Joanie's grandfather threw back his head and laughed. "Oh really? And why is that girl? Because you finally realized that I am famous?"

"No," Joanie rolled her eyes and shook her head, "I knew you were famous for your music and stuff and you made films. You are magical because you finally learned the healing power of love."

Joanie's grandfather looked down at her and his blue-gray eyes twinkled with moisture. Smiling he said at last, "You know what, Joanie? You are right, I did -- finally. About the time I realized the power of my own music."

Joanie took her grandfather's hand. "Come on. Let's go eat. I am starved. Did you find your veggie burgers?"

"No, they did have these great vegetable quiches though."

Joanie and her grandfather walked away from the memorial table hand-in-hand and as she looked around the room at all the people talking and laughing about a woman who had touched them so deeply, Joanie saw the healing power of love and the inspirational power of music as a very powerful combination indeed. Behind them, on the table, was a book, its cover splashed with neon restaurant signs and drumsticks and the title, "Where's Benjamin? A Story of Love & Healing in Music."

Joanie knew exactly where the drummer named Benjamin was located. He lived in the studio near her house and he was holding her hand. She silently thanked The Empress for bringing him back to the land of the living and the place of love and inspiration. The image of Wolf Stealer, his arms around his daughter and his wife, restored and powerful, came clear in Joanie's mind as though the past and the present were actually one. In that moment, she knew she could hear the beating of the tribe's heart next to her own, strong, clear, vibrant and a woman's voice, calm and melodic welcoming her to path of the shaman. The path of mystery and dreams.

Never Underdressed

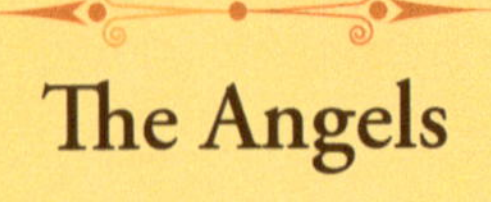

The Angels

Angels
Grasp me gently
Securely

Floating down
Cool waters
Sticks, detritus

Cram the bank
Float past
Eddy in pools of other dreams

Lush green branches
Lazy sun trickles
Warming joints

I am never cold
Gently we float
Angels whisper

Quiet soothing words
Releasing tension
I let go

II

Remembering distantly --
Deadlines
Stressful moments

Goodbyes
Meandering mistakes
Compounding anecdotes

Misaligned adventures
Miracles beyond my grasp

III

You are good enough
They whisper
We hold you always

Let us take you now
Instantly,
I perceive the river

Long and winding
Lifetime road
Destination sighted

Tensed muscles
Laundry lists
To dos

Down river
Light glows brighter
Music plays

Inviting cuisine
Scenting my palette --
We'll take you there

Your work is done
Nothing to do
Fantastic voices smile in my ear

Mind reels
Presuming some cruel joke
Who's so magnanimous?

Flashing prices
Predicaments
Thrashing

I gasp for air
My heart speaks quietly
Insistently

Light of the angels
Caressing
Soothing words

Accepting
Complete
Trial's boon

Swimming ever onward
Vestiges of my grip release
Angels command the waters

Refreshing
Questing
Destination sighted

IV

Smooth
Tantalizing breath
Visions –

Hot chocolate
Brie cheese
Jamaican hideaway

Ceasing disbelief
End in sight
Stop my fighting

Rapids tumble
Let it all go
Delectable

Crisp
Watery ride
Submissions complete

Two angels holding
No diamonds
Love

Light
Wholeness within
My grasp

Closing eyes
Take me home
Release.

February 2, 2005

www.ingramcontent.com/pod-product-compliance
Lightning Source LLC
Chambersburg PA
CBHW041128100726
47911CB00002B/74

* 9 7 8 0 5 7 8 0 4 7 0 1 0 *